GAUDÍ's
SAGRADA FAMILIA:
A MONUMENT TO NATURE

GAUDÍ's
SAGRADA FAMILIA:
A MONUMENT TO NATURE

Jordi Cussó i Anglès

editorial
MILENIO

Original text in Catalan:
Gaudí(r) de la natura
i de la Sagrada Família
© Pagès editors, 2010

© Text and photographs: Jordi Cussó i Anglès, 2010
© Drawings and photographs: Junta Constructora del Temple de la Sagrada Família, 2010
© Photographies on pages 39, 46 and 47: Institut Amatller d'Art Hispànic - Arxiu Mas, 2010
© of the translation: Ramon Sala Gili, 2010
© of this edition: Editorial Milenio
    C/ Sant Salvador, 8 - 25005 Lleida
    www.edmilenio.com
    editorial@edmilenio.com

First edition: october of 2010
2nd edition. Reprint: July 2011
ISBN: 978-84-9743-422-5
Legal deposit: L-770-2011
Printed in Arts Gràfiques Bobalà, S. L.

◁ imprès a **lleida** ▷

Printed in Spain

For Maisse and Neus, my wife and my daughter,
for their patience and support.

I thank the Construction Committee of the Expiatory Temple
of the Sagrada Familia, the archives, the technical office and
model shop of the T.E.S.F. Cátedra Gaudí, as well as
Joan Bassegoda, Jordi Bonet, Jordi Faulí, Jaume Cases,
Toni Caminal, Carles Farràs, Josep Gargallo, Teresa Martínez,
Marta Otzet, Anna Perarnau, Albert Portolés, Jordi Ramon,
Jaume Serrallonga, Josep Tallada, Eduard Turon, Laia Vinaixa
and Vidiella Flors.

Index

Introduction

*T*his book has two main objectives: to divulge the roots of Gaudí's organic architecture and to encourage the readers to go back in time and try to decipher that '*great book of nature*' as he used to say, searching for the geometry of the animal, mineral and vegetal realms. In other words: to look at nature through his eyes. After observing the environment in detail, Gaudí reached a synthesis of structure and form, easily visible in his mature works, especially in his last and most admired construction: the naves of the temple of the Sagrada Familia. As a guiding thread, it includes some of his observations (in italics), recorded by his disciples during long conversations in his studio and in the temple workshops.

After working for almost fifty years in the scale model workshop (thirty three of them in the place where Gaudi had his laboratory), surrounded by the original plaster models which were destroyed (along with his studio and workshop) in July of 1936 during the first days of the Spanish Civil War, with the collaboration of his past helpers, we have managed to restore the thousands of fragments of the original work, rendering it suitable for further study. A painstaking labour which has familiarized me with the process Gaudí probably followed, from the first Neo-Gothic project for a church to the last version of the temple naves, learning to understand the geometric surfaces that he so wisely employed. Especially the ruled surfaces, false planes or *planoids* —as Gaudí used to say—; comparing them with the richness of the natural forms. It was a pleasant study which led me to live in the middle of nature, taking care of a small garden. This book is the result of that enthralling investigation and its astounding findings. I want the reader to enjoy both Gaudí and nature, as has been my case since I first contracted the "Gaudí virus". And, please, do not vaccinate yourself against it before you start…

After having read the Intergovernmental Panel report on Climactic Change, where we are warned about more drastic and imminent alterations than it was first thought, it's clear that only we can change the progressive heating of the planet and its ultimate destruction —while there's still time— through our daily behaviour, by following the credo of love and respect for nature proposed by Gaudí.

I have an ambitious goal: to make a small contribution to the "Gaudinists" around the world —through talks, articles, seminars and other activities— who divulge the work of the Maestro. With a very clear aim: to stimulate and incite new generations of architects, technicians, designers and artists, towards the use of the superbly equilibrated natural forms that Gaudí identified and employed more than a century ago. "*It seems strange that I have been the first man to use them. To be original, you must return to the sources.*" Return to nature, breaking away from routine, by being original. Only in this way we can discover that "*great open book that one must strive to read: the Book of Nature.*" We must think positively, be humble and partake of the natural perfection and harmony, the result of millions of years of evolution. We mustn't forget that we also are part of it.

1852-1878. Childhood and schooling

Antoni Gaudí i Cornet was born on the 25th of June 1852 in Baix Camp (Tarragona), the fifth son of Francesc Gaudí i Serra, a native of Riudoms, and Antònia Cornet i Bertran, a native of Reus.

He was baptized the following day in the parish church of Sant Pere in Reus. There is only a record of his baptism, not of his birth, leaving unclear whether he was born in Reus or in Riudoms.

He was a frail baby who only a few months later, started suffering from rheumatism in the joints. Because of that he was never able to play with the other children and didn't go to school until quite late.

His infancy would turn out to be crucial to his future work, as his mother used the time she had to keep him by her side to teach him to observe the environment, the natural surroundings of the family home in Riudoms and of the Maset de la Calderera ("the boiler maker wife's little farm"), a place they visited regularly, full of trees, plants and animals. Gaudí would say of this place: *"That's where I got my most pure and pleasurable glimpses of nature."* Those images instilled an enormous interest, appreciation and respect for the environment and showed him the way towards his concept of a peculiarly organic 'naturalistic architecture', which he would develop in all his buildings.

The times he spent in his grandfather's workshop would also be very important for his development, as they were responsible for acquiring a sense of spatial vision, perhaps in a sense, innate. *"I am gifted with a sense of spatial perception, because I am the son, grandson and great grandson of coppersmiths."*

In 1860, he started his schooling with a teacher named Francesc Berenguer, who witnessed one of the first anecdotes we know about the child. When the teacher affirmed that the reason birds had wings was so that they could fly, Gaudí replied: *"The chickens at the farm have quite large wings but they do not fly."* In later years he would attend the school of Rafael Palau.

In the school year of 1863-1864, he went to the Piarists High School of Reus. He got all kinds of grades but made adequate progress until, in 1868, he transferred to the High School of Carme Street, in Barcelona. After graduation, he went on to the Architecture School of the same city.

From 1868 until 1878, he combined his studies with a paid job with several architects; he collaborated on several of Francesc de P. Villar i Lozano and Josep Fontserè i Mestres projects. He frequently visited the workshop of Eudald Puntí, where he learnt several trades (carpentry, blacksmithing and plaster modelling) under the guiding hand of some excellent artisans, such as the sculptor

Llorenç Matamala i Piñol who would be one of his most important collaborators in the construction of the Sagrada Familia. While still an undergraduate student he drafted a few private projects.

The interest, love and respect instilled in him by his mother during the first years of his life, a time when every child is like a sponge, were responsible for his life-long analytical observation of the environment. He felt the perennial human yearning for learning something new each day. After joining several hiking associations he made excursions around Catalonia with other hikers or alone. His constant reading of books borrowed from the school's library and the collecting of postcards from the world's different regions, helped to complete his naturalist formation.

He obtained his official title of architect on March 15th of 1878 and began working professionally, developing a new and original concept of building which, with the passage of time, would become his unique style.

MASET DE LA CALDERERA IN RIUDOMS
A view of the present building (smaller and with only one floor) constructed in 1922 on the land where the farm of his infancy stood.

MASET DE LA CALDERERA IN RIUDOMS
House built in 1922.

PEDESTAL OF THE NATIVITY FACADE
Pedestal with poultry; a reference to the Maset de la Calderera.

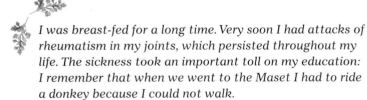

I was breast-fed for a long time. Very soon I had attacks of rheumatism in my joints, which persisted throughout my life. The sickness took an important toll on my education: I remember that when we went to the Maset I had to ride a donkey because I could not walk.

In later years, I started going to school with the teacher Berenguer and, after, with the teacher Palau.

ANTONI GAUDÍ

THE GAUDÍ HOME IN REUS
The house of Gaudí's maternal family in number 4 Sant Vicenç Street, where, on the ground floor, his grandfather's boiler-making workshop used to be.

THE ANCESTRAL HOME OF THE GAUDÍS IN RIUDOMS
In number 14 of Raval de Sant Francesc, recently restored.

As a result of my frailty, I had to abstain from participating in children's games, which pushed me to observe my surroundings. Once, when the teacher was explaining that birds had wings so they could fly, I said: 'The fowl on our farm have very large wings but they don't know how to fly; they use them to steady themselves when they run."

ANTONI GAUDÍ

Next to the flower pots, surrounded by vineyards and olive trees, cheered by the birds singing and the bugs buzzing, with the mountains of Prades as a backdrop, I became aware of the most pure and pleasurable images of Nature, that Nature which will always be my teacher.

ANTONI GAUDÍ

CORBEL WITH SWIFTS' NESTS
Family home of the Gaudís in Riudoms.

1878-1883. Gaudí, architect. First works

O nce he obtained the professional title of architect, Gaudí started work on several projects. One of them was the Workers Cooperative of Mataró, the capital of the Maresme region; a project he undertook with interest since it was one of the first cooperatives started in the country. He designed several buildings for it: the textile factory, the workers' homes and a social centre, the Casino, inside the same urbanization, which would be only partially built.

BLEACHING ROOM
A nave of the Workers Cooperative of Mataró, for which Gaudí designed a structure of twelve catenary arches in wood. A vintage photo.

STRUCTURE OF THE WAREHOUSE
In 2002, during the International Gaudí Year, the Mataró Town Hall undertook to restore the bleaching room. View of the restored arches in the summer of 2006.

In this project, we begin to find references to nature, such as the catenaries shaped arches, a curve frequently found in nature. I would like to underline the resorting to the bee as a symbol of laboriousness in one of the posters and in the flag's mast. In the case of the poster, Gaudí substitutes the word "Workers" for two bees toiling on a loom. In the same poster he drew a plant, a thistle (*Carduus sp.*), as a reference to the carding of wool, a way to comb impurities out of the fleece. Sometimes, dried burs were used for the same purpose.

CROWN OF THE FLAG'S MAST
The bee, a symbol of laboriousness: motif of Gaudí for crowning the flag's mast of the cooperative.

POSTER
In this poster of the Workers' Cooperative of Mataró, a drawing of some bees stands for the word "Workers".

The catenary arch

*I*n most of his buildings, Gaudí used catenaries, the curve adopted by a chain suspended from two points, more or less open depending on the distance between them.

Gaudí thought that when inverting this hanging curve he obtained a natural and perfect arch, aesthetically pleasing and with unbeatable mechanic properties, as it sustains itself by its own weight, without the buttresses required in other types of arches. We find them in his principal works: the Cooperative of Mataró, the Teresianas School, the stables and belvedere of the Güell Mansion, the attic of the Milà House, the main doors of the Güell Palace and even in the Sagrada Familia's naves.

It's a curve frequently seen in nature: in the vines hanging from two branches, cobwebs and in the strings of eggs spawned by toads.

Vines are tropical creepers that frequently hang between branches adopting the shape of catenaries.

The common toad, *Bufo bufo*, is an amphibian; the female spawns a string of eggs that she deposits in the water, where they form catenaries between the plants. In each string there can be between 1.000 and 6.000 eggs that will hatch within 12 days of being spawned.

Cobwebs are nets created by spiders by secreting a silken, flexible and very sturdy thread, from paired glands called spinnerets in the lower part of their abdomen. The wind blows them away until they stick to an obstacle; when they do, they form catenaries (which we tear apart when walking through them).

CATENARIES
The pull of gravity determines the shape (somewhat similar to a parabola) a chain adopts when you hang it from two hooks.

The force of gravity is radial (not parallel); therefore, a compressed catenary is a curve that closes itself towards the centre of the Earth, while an elongated one tends to raise itself indefinitely towards the sky. This means that it is a curve of transition between the ellipse (closed) and the hyperbole (open).

ANTONI GAUDÍ

VINES
Vines are creepers that describe catenaries between the jungle's trees.

STRINGS OF TOAD'S EGGS
The female toad deposits over the water strings of eggs that form a catenary.

SPIDER'S WEB STRING
Spiders are tireless spinners of catenaries.

The hyperbole, parabola and catenary are funicular curves; in the first one the main charge is in the centre and it decreases when the distance augments; in the second, the charge increases with the distance from the centre (that's the reason for the curve being between the parabola and the ellipse). A funicular is a paraboloid.

ANTONI GAUDÍ

Casa Vicens, in Carolines Street of Barcelona

In the spring of the year 1878, Manuel Vicens Montaner, a stockbroker, commissioned Gaudí, then a 26 year old architect, to build a house for him in Carolines Street of Gracia. The blueprints waited undisturbed for five years; the masons didn't start the task until 1883. Gaudí found the inspiration for this project in nature, putting all the observations he had gathered since he was a child to good use. All his life, he harboured the love and respect for the environment his mother had instilled in him, studying the flora and fauna and sketching what he saw, first in Tarragona and during his visits to the farm of Manuel Vicens in Alella or, later on, in his walks around Catalonia. When he went to draw a floor plan of the land where they were going to build the Casa Vicens, he found that it was covered by a large quantity of plants with yellow flowers, with a dwarf palm tree in its centre. He told himself: "*I will have to pull these plants before we start the construction, but I shall make them reappear in the exterior decoration of the house.*" Inside the building there is a splendid wave of naturalism; a décor of plants and animals spread on the walls and ceilings of every room, using different techniques and materials. Many of those papier-mâché decorative elements were constructed by Hermenegild Miralles. He even went as far as to hang a bird from a wire in front of a fireplace so that it would swing with the rising warm air.

CASA VICENS IN NUMBER 24 CAROLINES STREET IN BARCELONA
In 1878, Manuel Vicens i Montaner entrusted Gaudí with the project for his house, which was not started until 1883.

When I went to measure the plot, it was totally covered by a spread of little yellow flowers which were the inspiration for the form of the decorative tiles. I also found an exuberant Mediterranean fan palm. The cast iron pieces of the railing and the front grille mimic the shape of its leaves.

ANTONI GAUDÍ

MARIGOLD. *CALENDULA OFFICINALIS*
An annual plant that probably inspired the tiles Gaudí designed.

DECORATIVE TILES IN THE FACADE
Tiles with a design of small yellow flowers similar to the ones Gaudí found when he went to measure the plot.

MEXICAN MARIGOLD.
TAGETES ERECTA
Many experts believe that Gaudí reproduced these flowers in the tiles of Casa Vicens, although the leaves in them are much more similar to those of the marigold.

LEAF OF THE MEDITERRANEAN FAN PALM: THE MODEL FOR THE GRILLE
Original clay model made by the sculptor Llorenç Matamala i Piñol in the Sagrada Familia workshop. It can be seen in the Temple Museum.

MEDITERRANEAN FAN PALM (*CHAMAEROPS HUMILIS L.*)
A European palm tree spread through Catalonia and the Balearic Islands. The one in the plot of Casa Vicens inspired Gaudí's grille for the house.

 The great open book that one must strive to read is the book of nature; all the other books are extracted from it and contain man's erroneous interpretations. There are two revelations: one, doctrinaire, with Morals and Religion; the other, guided by facts, enclosed in the Great Book of Nature.

ANTONI GAUDÍ

MEDITERRANEAN FAN PALM LEAF IN CAST IRON
Grid of the cast iron grille made by the blacksmith Joan Oñós, based on the leaf of the Mediterranean fan palm, with marigold bracts in the corners.

Paintings, through the use of pigments, and sculptures turning to forms, express existing organisms: figures, trees and fruits... describing the interiors through the exteriors. Architecture creates the organism and that is what makes it adopt a law harmonious with those of nature; those architects that do not comply with this draw doodles instead of works of art.

Antoni Gaudí

MEDITERRANEAN FAN PALM LEAF
Palm leaf very similar to the Mexican palm (*Washingtonia robusta*).

21

1883. A remarkable year

Three of the projects started by Gaudí in 1883, we find outstanding. In February, he signed and submitted the blueprints for Casa Vicens, where the construction work started in October. In March, he started work on El Capricho of Comillas (Cantabria). And in November he took charge of the temple of the Sagrada Familia, whose crypt had been built by the architect of the diocese, Francesc de P. Villar Lozano.

BALCONY OF CASA VICENS
In the corners of the guard-rail of the first floor you can see the same tiles with sunflower motifs that Gaudí used in El Capricho of Comillas.

CAPITALS OF EL CAPRICHO IN COMILLAS
In the capitals of the columns at the entrance, you can see the leaves of the Mediterranean fan palm, which Gaudí also used as a motif for the grille of Casa Vicens.

For the exterior embellishment of both projects (Casa Vicens and El Capricho), Gaudí searched for inspiration in Oriental architecture and botanical figures, such as the leaves and heads of the sunflower (*Helianthus annuus*) and the leaves of the Mediterranean fan palm (*Chamaerops humilis L.*)

IRON COBWEB
A reproduction of the spider web with a pretty spiral shape, which can be seen in a window grille of Casa Vicens.

TILES WITH SUNFLOWER (*HELIANTHUS ANNUUS*) MOTIFS
They decorate the facades of El Capricho in Comillas (Cantabria) and the balconies of Casa Vicens in Carolines Street of Barcelona.

The cross of five limbs

In many of his works we find this five-armed cross, a shape typical of Gaudí, inspired perhaps by the fruit of "the tree of life", the cypress.

When the cones of the Mediterranean cypress (*Cupressus sempervirens*) open to release their seeds, they acquire a shape similar to the crosses Gaudí designed for the crowning tops on the Teresianas School, the house of Bellesguard, the guard's lodge in Parque Güell, Casa Batlló and (in the original project) the highest tower of the Sagrada Familia dedicated to Jesus.

THE CONE, FRUIT OF THE CYPRESS. *CUPRESSUS SEMPERVIRENS*
In a corner of the open fruit you can see the five arms similar to Gaudí's cross.

THE FIVE-ARMED CROSS
Crowning top of the tower of Bellesguard, probably inspired by the cypress' cones.

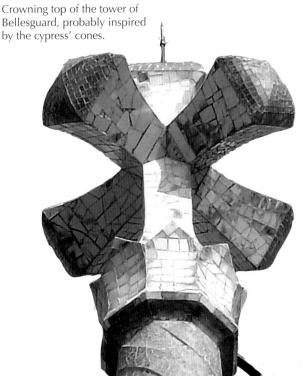

CYPRESS. *CUPRESSUS SEMPERVIRENS*
A perennial tree from the Cupressaceae family, with imbricated leaves and rounded cones.

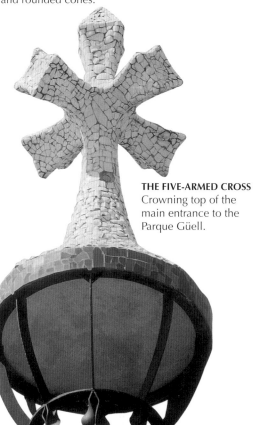

THE FIVE-ARMED CROSS
Crowning top of the main entrance to the Parque Güell.

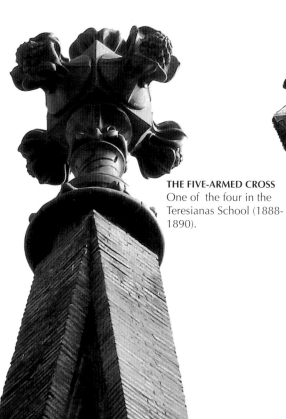

THE FIVE-ARMED CROSS
One of the four in the Teresianas School (1888-1890).

THE FIVE-ARMED CROSS
Crowning top of Casa Bellesguard (1900-1917).

1883. Gaudí, architect of the Sagrada Familia temple

In the year 1883, Gaudí took charge of the construction work of the temple, whose crypt had been started by Francesc de P. Villar. A short time later, when it was time to place the capitals on top of its columns, Gaudí decided to decorate them with botanical motifs: some enlarged endive leaves. These were the first naturalistic sculptures he used in the Sagrada Familia. In 1989, the crypt's vault was completed.

ESCAROLE . *CICHORIUM ENDIVIA* VAR. *CRISPA*
An herbaceous plant of the daisy family, with broad twisted leaves. It was much appreciated by the Egyptians, Greeks and Romans.

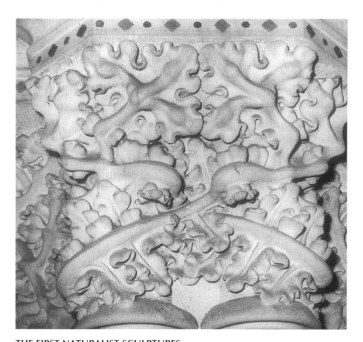

THE FIRST NATURALIST SCULPTURES
The capitals of the columns in the temple's crypt, where Gaudí reproduced large escarole leaves.

1889-1894. The apse

Once the crypt was finished, he continued with the apse wall (maintaining the Neo-Gothic style and following the structure of the crypt, made up of seven chapels and one nave on each side) and the staircase leading to the ground floor. From here until the high part of the apse (at approximately 30 m distance) he only finished the eastern part of the stairs, although he completed all the sculptured elements, such as the gargoyles (land snails), banisters with botanic decorations and the stone pinnacles in the shape of floral buds. These elements would not be incorporated into the building until 1978-1979. At midpoint in the columns of the chapels, in order to expel the rainwater coming down from the roof, Gaudí built gargoyles in the shape of amphibians and reptiles from Catalonia: fourteen beasts in total (toads, salamanders, lizards, snakes and others) with inner conducts in zigzag to reduce the speed of the stream that finally emerges from their mouths. In the front wall and pinnacles of the chapel we find a series of ears of wheat and of the anodyne wild plants that grew in the fields around the temple. Gaudí used to ask his collaborators to gather them so that the sculptors could model and cleave them out of the stone blocks. To decorate the banisters in the high part of the chapels he continued to rely on botanic motifs: branches of cypresses, cedars, fan palms, rosetrees, olives and others. A decoration he repeated in the exterior facades of the apse staircase, where we find snail-shaped gargoyles, a land snail in the West and a sea snail in the East. For crowning the pinnacles, he had the buds of several flowers sculpted in stone.

PINNACLES OF THE APSE
Those pinnacles at the top of the eastern staircase reproduce several flower buds highly enlarged.

The Temple will not have abutments. What could pass for one in the apse is only a dead weight to harmonize the bell towers that will be in each of the three facades. The pinnacles already rising in the apse are 50 m high, the bell towers that will be in the portico of the nativity will measure 100 m high, and the dome around 150 m. I have carried out some interesting experiments in the lab of the Industrial School. I apply a charge equivalent to one tenth of the fracture coefficient on all the materials I use.

ANTONI GAUDÍ

BANISTERS AND PINNACLES OF THE APSE
Banisters decorated with diverse botanic motifs and pinnacles with a reproduction of flower buds, at the end of the flight of stairs on the eastern side.

Architecture is the first of the plastic arts; sculpture and painting rely on it.

All its excellence comes from the light. Architecture is the arranging of light; sculpture is the play of light; painting is the reproduction of light through colours, which are the components of light.

ANTONI GAUDÍ

APSE WALL
In the pinnacles and the top of the wall of the seven chapels of the apse we find a series of stone reproductions of the ears of various grains and weeds.

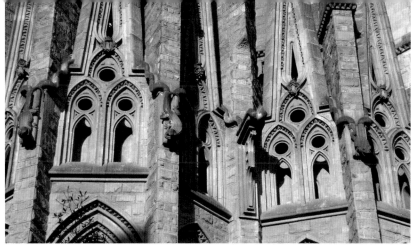

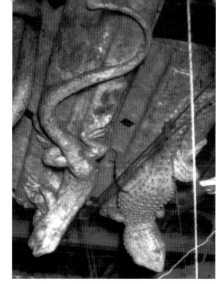

MODELS OF REPTILES
Plaster models hanging from the ceiling of Gaudí's studio-workshop as a guide for the stone sculptures.

GARGOYLES OF THE APSE
Fourteen gargoyles of the apse shaped like amphibians and reptiles common to Catalonia.

MONTPELIER SNAKE. *MALPOLON MONSPESSULANUS* (*Hermann, 1804*) Greenish venomous snake that can measure up to 2 m.; it's a typically Mediterranean species.

EUROPEAN COMMON GECKO. *TARENTOLA MAURITANICA* (*Linnaeus, 1758*) Small insectivorous and oviparous reptile, measuring around 9 cm, found all over Catalonia.

COMMON TOAD. *BUFO BUFO* *Linnaeus, 1758*) A sturdy amphibian that can reach 20 cm. It's common in Catalonia.

COMMON LIZARD. *TIMON LEPIDUS* (*Daudin, 1802*) It is the biggest lizard that can be found in Europe. It lives in Valencia and in many parts of Catalonia.

1894-1926. The Nativity Façade

FAÇADE OF THE NATIVITY
The central portico of the façade, with sculptures of the birth and infancy of Jesus, surrounded by stone reproductions of the local flora and fauna.

*A*fter finishing the seven chapels of the apse, Gaudí continued by building the two flights of stairs and laying the foundations of the Nativity façade.

In 1895, Gaudí set the bases of the two large columns dedicated to the Virgin Mary and Saint Joseph. They had the shape of two turtles and were the first sculptures of the façade of the Nativity: a marine turtle on the sea side and a land turtle on the mountain side. The construction work continued with the laying of the pedestals with representations of plants and fowl. We can assume that they brought back memories of Gaudí's childhood in the Maset de la Calderera of Riudoms. The arcade of this façade is divided into three portals with sculptured representations of the Nativity and the infancy of Jesus, surrounded by an apotheosis of nature. Isidre Puig Boada, a disciple of Gaudí and director of the works of the Sagrada Familia for many years, published a list of the fauna and flora elements reproduced in stone in the porticos of the Nativity Façade: 31 botanical species and 68 different types of animals. He probably did not enumerate each one, as it would require a whole book to detail all of them. In this book we will only study a few of them in depth.

FLORA AND FAUNA SCULPTURED IN STONE
In the arch of the central portico of the Nativity Façade you can see a large number of sculptures of plants and beasts.

BASE OF THE NATIVITY FAÇADE
In which we find plants and domestic fowl related to Christmas meals.

SCULPTURE IN THE NATIVITY FAÇADE
The loggerhead sea turtle, *Caretta caretta (Linnaeus, 1758)*, lives in the seas around Catalonia.

SCULPTURE IN THE NATIVITY FAÇADE
The Hermann's tortoise, *Testudo hermanni (Gmelin, 1789)*, is one of the very few herbivore reptiles. It used to live in the Mediterranean climate zone of Catalonia.

Frieze with the symbols of Jesus, Mary and Joseph

For the lower side of the lateral walls of the Nativity Façade, Gaudí designed a frieze with the symbols of the Holy Family, Jesus, Mary and Joseph depicted horizontally. The frieze evokes the hooks spread by creepers to get hold of a branch. The shape of the cross in Jesus' symbol is almost identical to the drawing of a passion fruit branch attributed to Gaudí.

BRANCH OF A PASSION FRUIT TREE
Pasiflora edulis with helicoidal hooks.

FRIEZE ON THE LEFT SIDE OF THE FAÇADE
In the lower part you can see the symbols of Saint Joseph, Jesus and the Virgin Mary, demarcated by two points.

FRIEZE ON THE RIGHT SIDE OF THE FAÇADE
In the lower part you can see the symbols of Saint Joseph, Jesus and the Virgin Mary, demarcated by two points.

THE VINE, A PLANT WITH HOOKS
Vine, *Vitis vinifera*. A creeper with helicoidally twisted hooks that coil around any support. It produces grapes.

Drawing attributed to Gaudí with a branch of the passion fruit tree, *Pasiflora edulis*, a creeper of the gender Passiflora.

A HOOK OF THE PASSION FLOWER TREE
A corkscrew hook like the ones designed by Gaudí for the freeze of the Nativity façade.

Detail of Gaudí's drawing of a passion fruit branch and the anagram of Jesus. The cross in the drawing is very similar to the one sculpted in the frieze of the Nativity façade.

SYMBOLS OF JOSEPH, JESUS AND MARY
Detail of the freeze with the anagram of the Holy Family.

The ruled geometry

Planoids, false planes or "cross-eyed" planes (as Gaudí called them).

*A*ll the architecture students knew, at least empirically, the ruled surfaces of complicated names (such as paraboloids, hyperboloids, conoids or helicoids), but very few dared to use them. Gaudí realized its architectonic interest and the great possibilities of their use in the construction of buildings. He started studying these surfaces in detail, collecting the information published in his time by architects, physicists, biologists and other scientists, such as the *Studies in Descriptive Geometry* of C. F. A. Leroy, published in 1855; the work of the German mathematician Karl Hermann Amandus Schwarz; the investigations of Ernst Heinrich Haeckel, who published a book (in 1866) about the morphology of organisms with a large number of illustrations of radiolarian, sponges and jelly fish; the work of the Scottish biologist and mathematician Arcy W. Thompson (author of *On Growth and Form*, published in 1917) on the helicoidal structure of plants, and many more

All this valuable information, coupled with his own study of the geometry of nature, led to Gaudí experimenting with the ruled surfaces in the crypt of Colonia Güell. Once he was satisfied by their validity, he decided to apply them in the Sagrada Familia. This was the beginning of the great change in the temple's project (the Second Model). In 1914, he interrupted the works in the Colonia Güell and refused to accept more commissions so that he could dedicate all his efforts to the Sagrada Familia, delving into the new organic architecture in depth. This would make him famous.

CHURCH OF THE COLONIA GÜELL
The vault of the entrance to the crypt, where Gaudí used the hyperbolic paraboloids, following the model of the Catalan domes.

CHURCH OF THE COLONIA GÜELL
The column of the portico of entrance to the crypt with brick nerves decorated with a series of very thin paraboloids in the form of dolphins jumping up in the air. It is reminiscent of an exuberant palm tree.

SECOND MODEL
Model of the naves with parabolic surfaces like the ones Gaudí used for the first time in the Colonia Güell.

SECOND MODEL
New project of the arches of the lateral naves of the temple, made after experimenting with ruled surfaces in the Colonia Güell.

To be original implies getting close to the origin; with two rulers and a string you can generate all kinds of architectural elements, conceive surfaces and build planoids (false planes). In the Temple of the Sagrada Familia, I have opted directly for the later.

ANTONI GAUDÍ

37

The conoid

*I*t is the surface engendered by a straight line moving along a given curve and a straight edge, keeping parallel to a plane.

One of the first ruled surfaces that Gaudí applied in the Sagrada Familia was the conoid. Curiously, he did so in two minor constructions, provisionally destined for services. The first, on the corner of Sardenya and Provença Streets, very near the apse and the provisional entry to the temple's crypt, relied on the conoid to make a roof for the warehouse of the studio-workshop, built in 1899. It leans on an already existing home for the chaplain. The other building projected with conoids (for the roof as well as for the enclosing walls) was the Provisional School, an institution meant to collaborate in the education of the quarter's children and adults. The building was erected on the sea side of the plot, near the spot destined for the Glory façade. The school was inaugurated on November 15th of 1909. It was a great contribution of Gaudí to the conception of a new organic architecture which he would develop during the last 12 years of his life. It would influence other great masters: Le Corbusier, Pier Luigi Nervi, Félix Candela and even Santiago Calatrava.

GAUDÍ'S STUDIO-WORKSHOP
First building with conoidal surfaces designed by Gaudí for his studio, which was used as warehouse for his models.

PROVISIONAL SCHOOL
A picture of the school in Gaudí's day, with its conoidal ruled surfaces.

The Parish Schools of Sagrada Familia

In the buildings of the parish schools of the Sagrada Familia, you can clearly see this geometry of conoidal surfaces so abundant in nature, in the vegetal realm as well as in the animal.

On the ground floor you find three intertwined hearts, probably symbolizing the Holy Family: Jesus, Mary and Joseph; in the three fountains of the playground the initials "J", "M" and "J" appear.* The conoidal brick walls that enclose the Spartan construction are generated by straight lines which follow the initial sinusoid floor plan, on one side, and a 10 x 20 m rectangle, on the other. The result is pleasing to the eye, extraordinarily stable and naturalistic at the same time. The roof consists of a very simple structure, visible from inside the three classrooms; a practical lesson that helps to understand the generation of a ruled surface. The structure consisted of a long double "T" beam in the centre, dividing in two the rectangular space, standing on three pillars at 5 m over the ground with the ends resting on the walls. The joints were reinforced with small corbels. A series of planks acting as generators, were resting on the beam at different angles, as a consequence of following the sinusoids at the other end of the top of the walls. The new conoidal surface was generated by covering all the structure with three layers of slim bricks, forming a perfect drain for rainwater, with alternative inclinations and extensions of the wall-plate acting as gargoyles to expel the water far from the outside walls. Gaudí paid for everything with his own funds. It seems it cost him 9.000 pesetas, about 54 euros.

That small building that Gaudí designed as a provisional school, can still be seen in the southern corner of the temple. It has been reconstructed three times: twice when it was deliberately burned in 1936 and 1939 and a third time when it was dismounted and moved to its present location, where in 2002 it was rebuilt with total fidelity to Gaudí's project so that the construction of the temple could continue unimpeded. When the Civil War ended it was used as a grade school until the 80s.

(*) Article published in the magazine *Temple* in March-April of 1985 under the title "The School of the Expiatory Temple of the Sagrada Familia", written by the architect Francesc de P. Cardoner i Blanch.

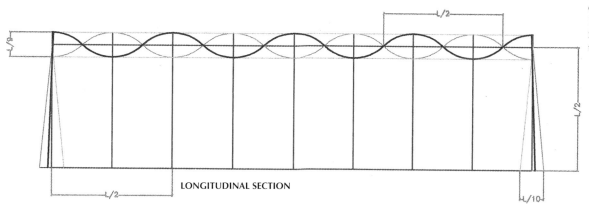

L/2

L/9

L/2

LONGITUDINAL SECTION

L/2

L/10

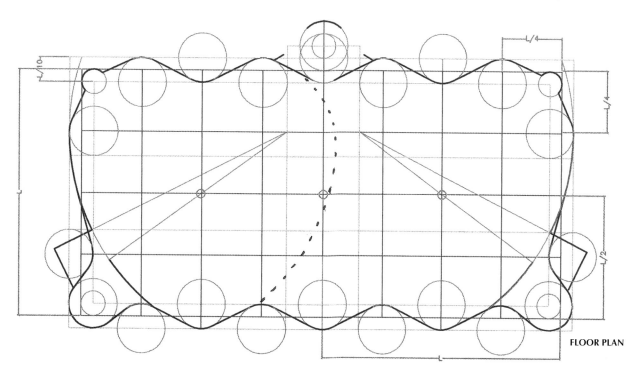

L/10

L/4

L/4

L

L/2

FLOOR PLAN

L

41

MAGNOLIA
Magnolia grandiflora
The magnolia leaves have a shape very similar to the conoids in the roof of the school buildings.

RULED SURFACES
Planoids or false planes in the walls and roof of the Parish Schools: forms frequently found in nature.

THE ROOF SEEN FROM THE INSIDE
As seen from the inside of the classrooms, this structure, helps to understand the generation of a ruled surface; a conoid, in this case.

FALSE ACACIA. *ROBINIA PSEUDOACACIA*
The winged seed of the false acacia, also called black locust, of an evident conoidal shape.

My aesthetic and structural concepts obey an "undisputable" logic. I have thought a lot about the fact that they have never been applied before, leaving it to me to do so for the first time. That's the only thing that could make me doubt. However, since I am convinced that they imply an improvement, I must use them.

Before I applied it to the Sagrada Familia, I used this structure in the Colonia Güell. Without this previous trial I would not have dared to use it in the Temple.

DETAIL OF THE ROOF
This is a conoidal surface where we can see a clear coincidence with natural shapes; especially those of the animal kingdom.

MANTA RAY. *MANTA BIROSTRIS*
The manta, or devilfish, is a large fish with pectoral fins from the Mobuloidea family.

Gaudí, also a pedagogue

In the new school, *Mosén* Gil Parés i Vilasau (as director), and Antoni Gaudí, (as designer) applied a pedagogic system which was very advanced for its time and acclaimed by many teachers. Their methods were later adopted by other educational centres that developed a more constructive way of teaching with a higher degree of participation from the pupils.

In his frequent visits to the dependencies of the Sagrada Familia and in several articles published in the magazine *Temple*, Josep Gargallo i Porta, a former pupil of the school, spoke to us of his experiences, tinged with good memories and a passionate nostalgia for those times. His recollections have aided us to contrast and complete our information about the Provisional Schools.

The school had three classrooms —with their corresponding playgrounds— prepared for teaching 150 children out in the open air. In every playground there was an area covered with heather extended over a metallic grille. Under this sort of lath house, the plastered walls doubled as blackboards. At the other end of the patio there were trees and *jardinières* with plants that the children grew, meant to instil in them the love and respect for nature, the feelings Gaudí cultivated since his infancy. In each playground there was a fountain adapted to the height of the children, with a thick and curved spout so that they could steady themselves when drinking water. Under them, there was a cylindrical basin with the appropriate depth for avoiding splatters.

In one of the playgrounds there was a round pond 30 cm. deep that was used for practical classes of Geography, where the pupils had fun using sand to reproduce the geographical incidents they had just studied.

Mention must be made of one of the pieces of furniture: the stools for giving classes out in the open. They were three legged so that they would remain steady on the ground. Another one was a practical four-sided gyratory cupboard where the class material was kept. As can be seen, Gaudí carefully designed all the details of this school, trying to make it as pleasing for the children as he could.

JARDINIÈRES AROUND THE BUILDING
In these *jardinières*, the pupils took care of the plants assigned to them.

FOUNTAINS IN THE PLAYGROUNDS
Fountain adapted for children, with a cylindrical sink to avoid splatters. The "M" stands for the Virgin Mary.

MEMORIES OF A FORMER PUPIL OF THE SCHOOL

Josep Gargallo i Porta studied in the Parish Schools from 1927 to 1935.

"In one of the playgrounds, Gaudí ordered that a round pond be built where we made maps and geographical features by rearranging the sand that was inside. Once done, we would let the water come in to simulate the seas. We used to call it 'The Geography Pond' and it was a fun way to learn the subject. Those of us who had the good luck of going to that school had no idea that our little building was a model for the ruled geometry discovered by Gaudí, a technical feat that was admired by the experts. We had more than enough with the additions, subtractions, straight lines and curves, to suspect that we were surrounded by conoids, paraboloids and hyperboloids.

GARDENING LESSON, 1913
It was meant to rouse the interest, respect and love of nature in the children.

GEOGRAPHY CLASSES
A cement pond in one of the school's playgrounds was used for practical lessons. In the background, on the right, the heather cover and the wall doubling as a blackboard can be seen.

Around the building he built *jardinières* with rough rocks, where each child had a plant assigned in order to awaken in him love and curiosity for nature. I felt sad when the school-year ended because my plant was going to wither."

The paraboloid

The paraboloid is a second degree surface that traces a parabola when it intersects a plane. There are variations, such as the paraboloid of revolution, the elliptic and the hyperbolic.

The hyperbolic paraboloid is one of the ruled surfaces used frequently by Gaudí. After experimenting successfully with them in the church of the Colonia Güell he recurred to them for the Sagrada Familia.

If you imagine a riding saddle with its perimeter prolonged ad infinitum, where the two curves, placed perpendicularly to each other, are two parabolas (concave and convex, respectively), you will have a paraboloid.

Gaudí searched for a way to make the uneducated masons the generation of these ruled surfaces, so that they could build paraboloids without erring. Quite cleverly, from the large parabolic surface he extracted a square where the four sides were generating lines and one of the vertexes was in a different plane from the rest. Those generators converted themselves into four guidelines that could be used to rest the straight line generated by the surface, following a distribution established in equal parts on the square's sides.

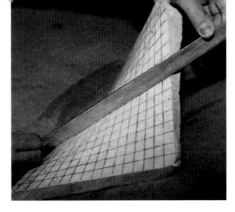

MODEL OF A PARABOLOID
A plaster model of a paraboloid with the generators in both directions marked, giving rise to a ruled surface.

CROCOSMI. *CROCOSMIA CROCOSMIIFLORA*
Crocosmias have leaves that grow in a parabolic shape.

The same way that three straight lines form a surface, three surfaces form a volume. Its faces are two planes and a planoid; i.e. a hyperbolic paraboloid.

ANTONI GAUDÍ

Building advantages of hyperbolic paraboloids.

When I first conceived the arches as hyperbolic paraboloids, I didn't dare to apply them because it had never been done before, but since this should not be an obstacle (otherwise, how there would ever be progress?), I tried them first in the Colonia Güell. In view of the good results there, I decided to use them in the Sagrada Familia.

I insist on the fact that those arches are only a wall in which the steering lines are not parallel; to build them, a mason needs only two rulers and a string, just like when he erects any wall. He thinks he is building a flat surface but he ends up with one that's "cross-eyed" or warped.

ANTONI GAUDÍ

SECOND MODEL
The arches and capitals of the lateral naves with hyperbolic paraboloids, a ruled surface that Gaudí decided to use in the Sagrada Familia, after verifying its good results in the Colonia Güell.

PARABOLOIDS IN THE HAND
The skin creases between the fingers of the hand trace some paraboloids.

The Passion façade

When he designed this façade, Gaudí opted for ruled surfaces. All over the façade one finds hyperbolic paraboloids, in the architectonic elements of the arches, the vertical girders and borders of the entry porticoes, the different loggias of the porch back wall and especially in the columns, the six large leaning ones delimiting the porch's space and the eighteen of the monumental frontage; all of them with diverse references to nature.

DRAWING BY GAUDÍ
The Passion Façade at a scale of 1:200.

KAPOK. *CEIBA PENTANDRA*
The kapok is a very large tree from Central America. Its trunk emerges from the ground forming parabolas.

BASE OF A COLUMN
The base of one of the columns of the façade's portico, with parabolic stones similar to the trunks of some trees.

SEQUOIA. *SEQUOIADENDRON GIGANTEUM*
A tree from Northern California also called redwood. Its trunk naturally describes parabolas.

The hyperboloid

Is a quadric structure with hyperboles on its flat sections.

The hyperboloid of one sheet is a ruled surface of revolution, generated by the rotation around a symmetry axis of a hyperbole or a leaning straight line. In some of his works, Gaudí used the hyperboloid of revolution: in the dome of the stables of the Finca Güell, the capitals of many columns inside the Palace Güell, the tower of the service pavilions or the central column for the grotto to park the carriages at the entrance of Parque Güell. He used it especially when projecting the temple's naves, where he transformed the bay windows of the First Model into more naturalist structures, resorting to hyperboles crossing each other (enhancing the entry of the light rays), sliding like generators over the ruled surfaces. Reaching the apex of his use of ruled geometry, Gaudí designed the ultimate solution for the lateral and central naves' arches, by combining the solid hyperboloids of revolution (as capitals for the columns) with a series of hollow hyperboloids of different sizes to admit the daylight and the nocturnal artificial lighting.

As is the case of the other ruled surfaces, the hyperboloids also have a reference in nature.

HYPERBOLOID OF ONE SHEET
Hyperbolic surface engendered by straight lines that describe a hyperbole in all the vertical and radial sections of the axis.

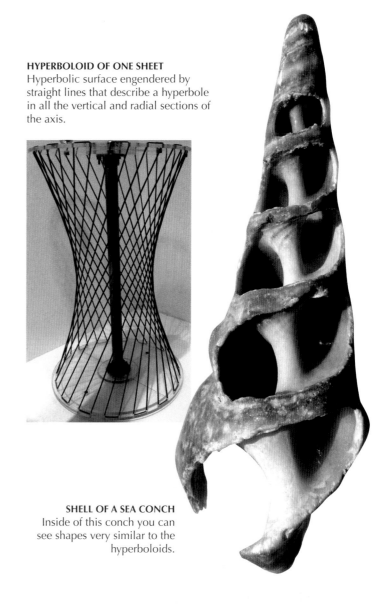

SHELL OF A SEA CONCH
Inside of this conch you can see shapes very similar to the hyperboloids.

THE CLOISTER FAÇADE

In the definitive solution to the cloister façade, we can see a triangular rosette with ten hyperbolic openings, very similar to the shell of the foraminifera.

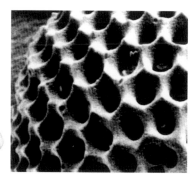

MICROPHOTOGRAPH OF A FORAMINIFERA

Test or calcareous shell of the foraminifera of the Protozoa order and the Rhyzaria group. This species has only one chamber with numerous hyperbolic openings from which a pseudopodial net emerges, as if it was a set of generators of hyperboloids.

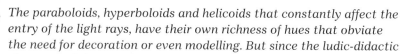

The paraboloids, hyperboloids and helicoids that constantly affect the entry of the light rays, have their own richness of hues that obviate the need for decoration or even modelling. But since the ludic-didactic character of the temple of the Sagrada Familia renders indispensable the symbolic and figurative representations of an ornamental entourage that frames them, I dive headlong on the search for a solution to the problems of the architectonic sculptures.

ANTONI GAUDÍ

DOME OF THE CENTRAL NAVE
Hyperbolic dome of the central nave, extraordinarily similar to the skeleton of a radiolarian.

MICROPHOTOGRAPH OF A RADIOLARIAN
Skeleton of a radiolarian of the Protozoo order and the Rizaría group, with small hyperbolic openings. In the intersections we can see a series of small teeth very similar to the protuberances of the hyperboloids in the naves' domes.

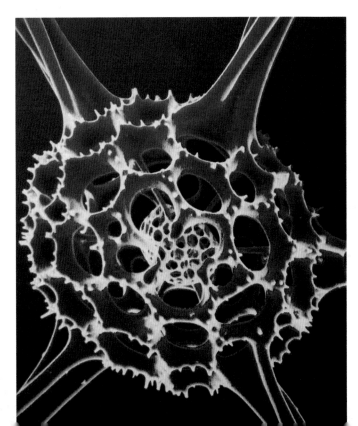

DOMES OF THE TEMPLE'S NAVES
Final solution to the domes of the lateral and central naves, with a combination of hyperboloids of one sheet and hyperbolic paraboloids.

The paraboloids, hyperboloids and helicoids are ruled surfaces; one leads into the other without interruptions.

ANTONI GAUDÍ

Gaudí, an arquitect with direct connections to the Universe

It would seem that the Universe began with a colossal deflagration, the so called Big Bang, thousands of millions of years ago. The stars appeared afterwards and, later, as a result of their bunching together, the galaxies. The Milky Way is the galaxy that contains the Earth. As is the case in many other galaxies, it has a revolving spiral shape. It's formed by five arms containing millions of stars. At the end of one of these arms you find our Solar System. To Gaudí, a keen observer of nature, the essence of architecture had to be intimately related with the geometry generated by the

OAK FRAME
Frame of carved oak wood with a portrait of Antoni Gaudí from Casa Calvet, exhibited in the Museum of the Parque Güell, with spirals in relief. Curiously, those on the upper side (N) turn counter clockwise, while the ones in the lower side (S) do so clockwise.

movement of the galaxies, the stars and the planets; especially ours, the Earth.

Gaudí said, "*Originality consists of returning to the origins.*" In the decoration of many of his works (the walls and ceilings of Casa Milà, the ceilings and banisters of Casa Batlló, the tiles of Casa Calvet or the dragon's tail of the Finca Güell) he used the spiral shape profusely.

As a planet of the Solar System, the Earth moves through the void in a translation movement around the Sun in addition to turning around its own axis; this last movement, seen from the Northern Hemisphere is counter clockwise and the other way around when observed from the Southern Hemisphere. This is something that can be deducted by the oscillation of a Foucault's pendulum, the direction of the prevailing winds or the circulation of the sea's streams. The result of it, coupled with the attraction of gravity, provokes a tendency towards a helicoidal movement. We find many examples of it in both in the vegetal and animal domains: shells of snails, horns and the movement of growing in plants, where the photoperiod (amount of light received per day) stimulates the growth in a certain direction.

Here we have a few examples of the natural tendency towards a helicoidal growth that Gaudí used in all his works (convinced that it was a movement that because of its equilibrium generates a great stability), especially in the construction of the Sagrada Familia.

An extraordinary spiral inside a sliced conch of a *Nautilus pompilius*.

A GENISTA POD. *SPARTIUM JUNCEUM*
When it splits to drop the seeds, it twists helicoidally in both directions.

57

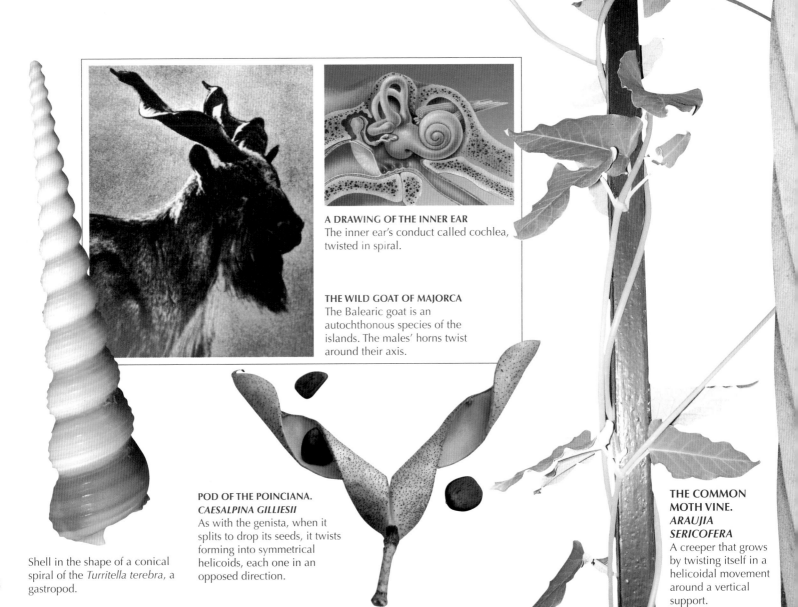

A DRAWING OF THE INNER EAR
The inner ear's conduct called cochlea, twisted in spiral.

THE WILD GOAT OF MAJORCA
The Balearic goat is an autochthonous species of the islands. The males' horns twist around their axis.

POD OF THE POINCIANA.
CAESALPINA GILLIESII
As with the genista, when it splits to drop its seeds, it twists forming into symmetrical helicoids, each one in an opposed direction.

THE COMMON MOTH VINE.
ARAUJIA SERICOFERA
A creeper that grows by twisting itself in a helicoidal movement around a vertical support.

Shell in the shape of a conical spiral of the *Turritella terebra*, a gastropod.

The Gaudí column. GCV. Generation-Growth-Plant

*A*ll throughout his professional life, the search for the ideal column was one of Gaudí's challenges. It was an investigation process that became obvious in the design of the columns of all his projects, in the shafts as well as in the capitals, where Gaudí mimicked the natural helicoidal growth of the plants.

Since 1883, when he became the architect of the temple of the Sagrada Familia, Gaudí intensified his search and with the help of an exceptional team of architects, draughtsmen and model makers, he began a new project especially centred on the study of the naves' columns, carrying out infinity of tests with plaster models in the temple workshop.

MODEL 1:10 IN GAUDÍ'S STUDIO, 1922-1923
In this picture you can see the process of definition of the column of helicoidal growth in two directions. On the left side of the model we see a great diversity of Solomonic columns (twisting in only one direction) of triangular section, with ridges more or less softened by parabolic curves; at right, we see the first versions of the column inspired by the natural growth of plants, with a double helix in both directions.

To reach a complete solution for the columns, we have spent 4.000 duros (about 200 €) and two years of intense and stubborn labour.

This is something that shouldn't seem strange, since the architectonical solutions have required the effort of many generations over a large number of lifetimes, and enormous amounts of money.

When you examine carefully the new styles, you find that they include previous forms but with many other details that make them superior to the classical solutions. Even if books are an instrument of culture based on facts, it's better to study directly from nature; from it we learn that things resolve their forms in the same sense that they are resolved in the Temple: that's the fundamental reason of it.

ANTONI GAUDÍ

Trees were the first constructions of nature.

This is something that was very clear to Gaudí. When he received visits in his studio, he would point to a large eucalyptus outside the window and he would say: "*That great tree is my teacher.*"

COMPARATIVE TABLE OF A TREE AND THE ARBOREAL COLUMNS OF THE TEMPLE'S NAVES IN THE SAGRADA FAMILIA

Roots	=	Foundations
Trunk	=	Column
Knots	=	Capitals
Branches	=	Small columns above
Foliage	=	Dome or roof of a construction

A construction is meant to offer us shelter from the sun and rain: in this it imitates trees, a natural refuge against storms.

The imitation reaches the elements, as the columns were first tree trunks and the capitals, the leaves. It's one more justification of the structure of the Sagrada Familia.

ANTONI GAUDI

Near Gaudí's studio, on the corner of Provença and Sardenya Streets, there used to be a tree.

The tree: one of the first natural constructions protecting us from the sun and the rain.

60

Several experimental versions

n the research on helicoidal growth, the Solomonic column is a constant. Gaudí turned to it in many of his projects: the façade of the Teresianas School (behind the community's coat of arms), the façade and lobby of Casa Calvet, several columns of the Parque Güell, the bases, central rings and capitals of the columns in the main lounge of Casa Batlló and other places. The temple of the Sagrada Familia is where Gaudí applied the results of his investigations most intensely.

PARQUE GÜELL
Columns with a helicoidal movement.

CASA CALVET
Solomonic column of the tribune.

The first temple's columns

For the Nativity façade, Gaudí designed a peristyle divided by three porticos with archivolts sustained by two large columns dedicated to Saint Joseph and the Virgin Mary, with two turtles in the base (a marine turtle on the side of the sea and a land turtle on the side of the mountain) and the capitals in the shape of palm leaves and fruit (dates). As a contrast to this naturalism, Gaudí transformed the palm's trunk into a cylindrical shaft with helicoidal ridges, one turning in the direction of the façade and the other away from it. In the central part of the peristyle, we find a third column dedicated to Jesus, in the shape of a bunch of palm leaves tied with a ribbon with His genealogy and a helicoidal growth counter clockwise. The façade was built slowly; in the lower part and the capitals of the columns of the windows of the different floors, the Maestro kept experimenting with the idea of imitating the natural geometry of a plant's growth, designing a series of different capitals with spiral ridges turning in both directions. On the mountain side of the same façade, to light the Rosary portico in the first stretch of the cloister, Gaudí built a lantern crowned by a pinnacle inspired by the floral bud of the aloe, sustained by eight columns with very beautiful geometric grooves, thus completing his study of the helicoidal growth of plants.

COLUMN IN THE NATIVITY FAÇADE
Column dedicated to Saint Joseph, with ascending helicoidal grooves turning to the left.

COLUMN IN THE NATIVITY'S FAÇADE
Column dedicated to Jesus, with an ascending ribbon coiled up helicoidally towards the right. It was installed in 1896.

COLUMN IN THE NATIVITY'S FAÇADE
Column dedicated to the Virgin Mary, with helicoidal grooves ascending towards the right.

Lantern of the cloister over the Rosary's portico

A study of the helicoidal growth of the plants, with eight different columns.

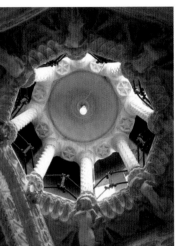

THE LANTERN OF THE CLOISTER ABOVE THE ROSARY PORTICO
It includes eight ridged columns with different geometric motifs of helicoidal growth.

THE PINNACLE OF THE LANTERN
The pinnacle inspired by botanic forms with an aloe bud (*Aloe arborescens*).

ALOE. *ALOE ARBORESCENS*
A perennial plant from the Asphodelaceae family with colourful inflorescences that bloom around Christmas.

COLUMNS WITH DIFFERENT GEOMETRIC MOTIFS

Process of elaboration of the column's shaft shape

First Model. 1883-1915

In the first Neo-Gothic project, the columns of the nave had a round section with a diameter of 1.05 m; in other words, the shaft of the first columns was cylindrical and smooth, without any drawings.

Second Model. 1915-1920

Here, Gaudí introduced an important change: the shaft's section became triangular, with a Solomonic growth. The Maestro progressed towards more organic forms, such as those of the trunks and branches of the trees. For the first fundamental change in the columns, especially those of the lateral naves, he used a twist of different intensities in diverse directions.

He modified the triangular section with different solutions, first rounding the ridges with small parabolas and, then transforming the straight sides of the triangle with three parabolas that softened and modified the frailty of the sharp angles of the equilateral triangles.

Gaudí kept experimenting with an identical generation applied to square or hexagonal sections (those of the columns of the central nave).

Third Model. 1920-1926

Gaudí reached the conclusion that the ideal column was the one generated by the double movement of translation and rotation in both directions, as natural as the growth of the plants. The fruit of all those years of research was the GGV column.

The model makers of the workshop began working with this new order which eventually became the definitive one, after initially trying different templates. As with the Second Model, they began with a triangular section and continued with a hexagonal one with sides slightly concave which was used in the support column of the choirs. They also experimented with an initial template in the shape of a convex hexagon made by six arcs of a circumference. It seems that this trial didn't please Gaudí, who continued experimenting with different polygons —square, rectangular and pentagonal— and, later, with starred polygons with six, eight, ten and twelve points, the result of symmetrically combining two triangles, two squares, two pentagons and three squares. The polygonal templates of the columns on the ground floor of the temple were softened with convex and concave parabolas, rounding the corners and filling up the inner angles, as a consequence of the geometry generated by the section of some paraboloids at their bases. At the level of the lateral naves' choirs and of the capitals of

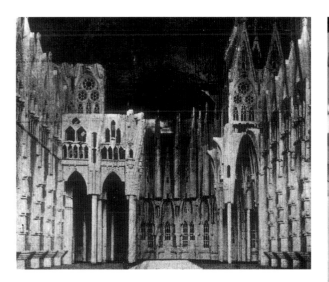

THE FIRST MODEL
The Neo-Ghotic project with cylindrical columns.

the central naves, all the polygons exhibit sharp ridges which grant the higher columns a greater relief and, therefore, more shadow.

In the naves of the temple, the complete order can be seen.

THE SECOND MODEL
With Solomonic columns of triangular section and domes with hyperbolic paraboloids.

THE THIRD AND FINAL SOLUTION
In the last 6 years of his life, Gaudí developed the column generated by a double helicoidal movement, the natural movement of growth in plants.

The definitive solution to the Gaudí column. 1920-1923

Gaudí and the phyllotaxis (the study of the arrangement of leaves on a shoot)

In the pile of Gaudí's original plaster models destroyed in 1936 at the beginning of the Spanish Civil War, they found a piece that was the key to understanding the years he spent studying the growth and disposition of a plant's leaves, especially those of the abelia (*Abelia floribunda*) and the oleander (*Nerium oleander*), the most similar to the model in question. Drawing on his studies, Gaudí began to develop the definitive solution to the temple naves.

ORIGINAL GAUDÍ MODELS
Archive of thousands of fragments of the original Gaudí's models, in the workshop of the Sagrada Familia.

ORIGINAL MODEL OF THE GROWTH OF PLANTS
A model of the study of the growth of plants that was basic in the development of the definitive solution to the Gaudí column.

OLEANDER. *NERIUM OLEANDER*
A perennial bush of the Apocinaceae family reaching up to 4 m, with leaves growing in alternate bunches of units of three. It grows along the entire Mediterranean coast and is often planted in public gardens and the central reservations of highways.

ABELIA. *ABELIA CHINENSIS*
Is a small bush of the Caprifoliceae family that can reach a height of 150 cm. It's a sturdy pollution-resistant plant, usually planted in urban environments.

They grow in an ascending helix in both directions around the shaft and the branches to gain a maximum exposure to the sun's rays. Seen from above, when you connect the apexes of the leaves in each of the groups with three straight lines, you obtain several equilateral triangles which turn 60° in a double (right and left) ascending helicoidal movement. The lower ones are inscribed within a cylinder, and the higher ones, inside of a cone (as a result of the gradual growth of the leaves). This movement is a reaction to certain stimuli of the environment, such as light, temperature, the pull of the gravity or the Earth's rotation around its axis: the tropisms. They can be positive or negative, depending on whether they act in favour or against the direction of the stimulus. In oleander, it's a phenomenon that presents a surprising particularity. The pith inside its branches has the same geometric shape as a Gaudí column of triangular base, since due to the helicoidal process of growth in both directions of the leaves, halfway the triangle converts itself into a hexagon, describing a 60° turn. On the other hand, we have the drawing of a passion fruit branch made by Gaudí, where he framed a group of three leaves with an equilateral triangle; significant proof of his interest for the growth and disposition of the leaves in a plant.

ABELIA. *ABELIA CHINENSIS*
Its leaves grow in groups of three to receive the maximum amount of light on their surfaces.

VIEW FROM ABOVE OF THE ABELIA
In some branches of the abelia (*Abelia chinensis*), the leaves grow in groups of three, describing equilateral triangles that turn 60° in an upward helicoidal movement in both directions.

If we compare the original model of Gaudí with an abelia or an oleander shoot, we can see that it is an exact copy of the distribution in groups of three of the leaves of those plants, enclosed by equilateral triangles. The surfaces between the different triangles' drums are generated by the intersection or 'twinning' of two helicoids that describe a 60° turn in two inverse directions at once. If we make a horizontal cut at the middle point of the trajectory between the triangles, the section transforms itself in a regular hexagon: the compressed column of Gaudí with a triangular base. From then on, the generation of a new column is solved; by just changing the initial template, the length and the amplitude of the turn (depending of the number of ridges or sides of the polygons), Gaudí defined the whole series of columns in the nave.

A COMPUTER 3D DRAWING
A computerized elevation of Gaudí's original model, where you can see the great geometric similitude to a shoot of the abelia.

A reproduction of Gaudí's model, cut in the middle of a drum, where a regular hexagon appears as a result of the intersection of the surfaces generated by the helicoidal growth in both directions of the original triangle.

A COMPUTER 3D DRAWING
A computerized cross section of Gaudí's original model employed for the development of the definitive solution to the columns of the temple naves. You can clearly see the generating geometry of the growth of the plants, with two helixes ascending in both directions, circumscribing the corners of the triangles.

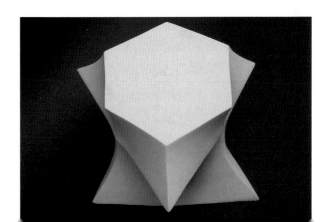

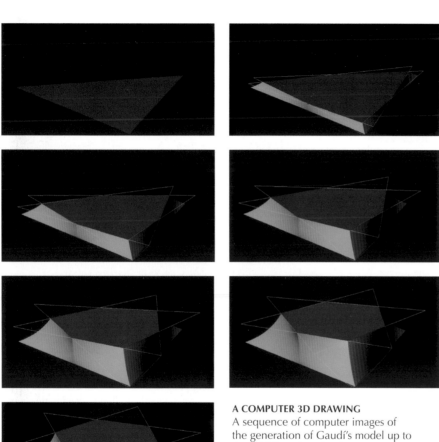

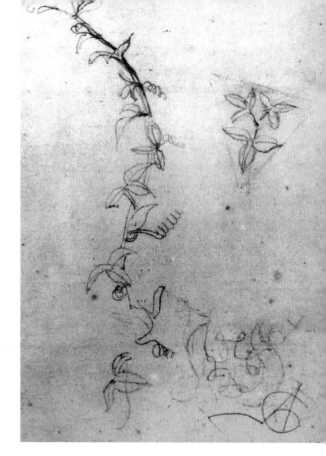

A COMPUTER 3D DRAWING
A sequence of computer images of
the generation of Gaudí's model up to
the middle point of a drum.

A drawing of a passion
flower branch (*Pasiflora
edulis*) attributed to Gaudí.
This plant is from the
Plassifloraceae family.

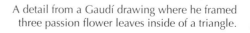

A detail from a Gaudí drawing where he framed
three passion flower leaves inside of a triangle.

A great discovery. A Gaudí's column inside of a branch

THE GREAT DISCOVERY

Gaudí's column with a triangular base, inside of an oleander branch (*Nerium oleander*). Plaster model of the pith of an oleander branch, where through the process of helicoidal growth of the leaves in both directions, the initial triangle transforms itself into a hexagon. It's the same generation found in all the temple's columns.

A SECTION OF AN OLEANDER BRANCH

A SECTION OF AN OLEANDER BRANCH
When you cut an oleander leaf near
the knot with the three leaves, you
can see the triangular shape of its
pith.

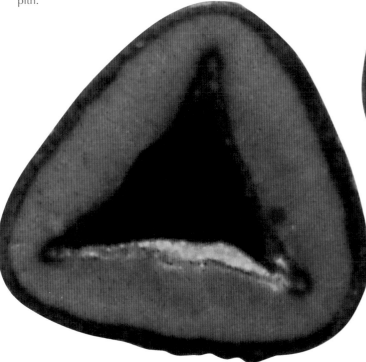

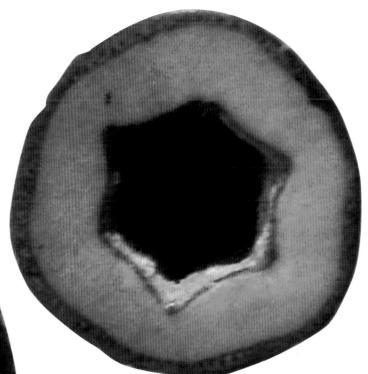

A SECTION OF AN OLEANDER BRANCH
At the midpoint between knots,
the pith of the oleander adopts a
hexagonal shape.

The first models of the new GCV column of Gaudí

Once he discerned the concept of the new column, Gaudí began testing it on plaster models.

We believe that the first columns generated by the double movement of translation and rotation in both directions of the initial templates, were those of the lateral naves above the choirs, built at a 1:25 scale, following the arboreal system of a trunk with four branches. The initial template of the four small columns (the branches) has the form of a triangle, curiously equal to the original model of the study of a plant's growth, rescued from vandalism in 1936.

FIRST MODELS OF THE GAUDÍ'S COLUMN
The first versions of the columns generated with a procedure similar to the natural growth of plants, in a model from Gaudí's studio.

EUROPEAN NETTLE TREE. *CELTIS AUSTRALIS*
A tree from the Ulmaceae family that is abundant in the vicinity of the temple. You can observe the similitude with the group of five columns that Gaudí designed for the lateral naves of the Sagrada Familia.

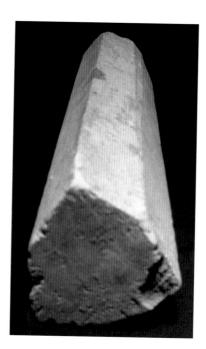

A SMALL ORIGINAL COLUMN IN THE STYLE OF A BRANCH
A fragment of the column with a triangular base, where we can observe how Gaudí eliminated a part, probably in order to allay the sharpness of the equilateral triangle's corners. In this section, the new edges that will become a regular hexagon start growing as a result of the generating movement in both directions.

AN ORIGINAL MODEL OF A COLUMN IN THE STYLE OF A TRUNK

An original model of the columns above the choirs, at a scale of 1:25, where you can clearly see the building process and the materials employed by the model makers of that epoch. A wood axis sustains a series of zinc templates, cut following the drawings of the sections generated by the movement in both directions of the initial module.

So many years of investigation finally achieved a result: a new column, "the Gaudí column".

The entire process has been documented in the temple's archives, with many photographs made in Gaudí's studio-workshop and a large quantity of plaster models, recuperated after restoring the originals destroyed at the beginning of the Spanish Civil War.

TREE GERMANDER. *TEUCRIUM FRUTICANS*

A plant from the Lamiaceae family frequently planted in gardens. The shoots usually present a square section, although sometimes the cut is hexagonal. You can see that some of the shoots twist helicoidally.

THE ORIGINAL COLUMNS USED IN THE PROCESS OF INVESTIGATION

Three columns made in Gaudí's workshop as part of his investigation process. On the left we see a Solomonic column of square section with the edges softened, ascending towards the right. In the centre we find a demonstration of the double turn of a convex hexagonal template, formed by six circumference arcs. On the right, another column of double turn with hexagonal template, with slightly concave sides and softly rounded edges. This column is very near the final solution; it only lacks the base.

The eight point column of the central nave

Once he had solved the generation of the new column, Gaudí began testing different initial templates, following the helicoidal growth in double directions. He experimented with a square, a rectangle, a pentagon, a hexagon and, later on, with polygons of six, eight, ten and twelve points, resulting from twinning two triangles, two squares, two pentagons or three squares.

For the load columns of the central nave and part of the lateral ones, Gaudí used the eight-point polygon (made of two symmetrically superimposed squares), with concave and convex parabolas softening the ridges and filling up the interior angles. Once the initial template was determined, he only had to follow the process of helicoidal growth in both directions of the plants until he arrived at another regular template; in this case, a template of sixteen sides softly undermined by the parabolas of the former. This same double turn procedure was applied to every template of symmetric polygonal profile, doubling the sides and ridges (32, 64, 128 and so on) until arriving at a polygon very close to a circumference.

All the naves' columns were generated in this way, changing the initial template according to the number of sides or ridges of the polygons and the height.

THE EIGHT POINT COLUMN
Column of the central nave generated by a helicoidal growth in double direction.

THE BASE OF THE EIGHT POINT COLUMN
Base of 80 cm. generated by a set of head-to-toe paraboloids that, when sectioned, draw an initial of the double helicoidal movement of the central nave's column. Something similar to the way the trunk of a tree grows.

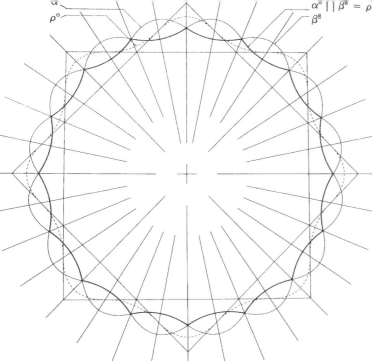

$\alpha^{\circ} \mid \mid \beta^{8} = \rho^{8}$
β^{8}
ρ°

A drawing of a template with a 16 sided polygon obtained by the double helicoidal turning of an eight point starred template. This section clearly resembles that of a Doric column.

A drawing of an initial template of two superimposed squares, forming an eight-pointed star, with ridges and inner angles softened by concave and convex parabolas.

The stars follow an orbit that is the trajectory of its equilibrium. In addition to this, they turn in a helicoidal movement.

The Sagrada Familia columns follow an axis of force that is the trajectory of its stability, its equilibrium. They are generated by a star section that turns as it ascends; its movement, therefore, is also helicoidal (as in the trunk of a tree). The stars come and go, since their orbits are closed curves. The column goes and comes back because it has a double helicoidal movement; it turns in both directions.

The decoration of the columns (of any style) is based on the application of this law, to a lesser or greater degree.

ANTONI GAUDÍ

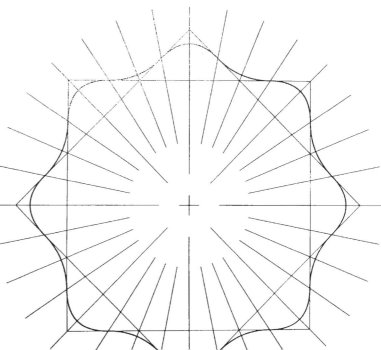

Inside the temple: a great forest

The supporting structure inside the temple's naves imitates the functioning of a tree, with trunk, branches and foliage through which the sunrays filter. At night, a set of spotlights mimics the starry firmament. The visitor has the impression of being in the middle of a forest.

This innovative organic architecture, a synthesis of form and structure is the result of a whole life of investigation that Gaudí spent passionately deciphering the great book of nature. When he finished the model, he lamented that he wouldn't live long enough to see a portion of the nave erected. Something that we are privileged to admire; the Sagrada Familia temple boasts completely finished naves, and its museum. We can see many of the original models approved by Gaudí, which were drawn from the blueprints for the continuation of the works.

The temple's interior will be like a forest. The naves' very structure tends towards that; the similitude appeared unintentionally. The pillars are helicoidal and slightly leaning. Helicoidal, because that's the proper form for the support of a charge above, and leaning, since that is the direction of the discharging of the forces transmitted by the nerves of the arches and the domes. At the level of the lateral naves, the supports split into four pillars —like the branches of a tree— and a fifth one that, as a guide, shoots up to the domes. The leaning pillars of the triforium look like the branches of a colossal tree.

The décor of the domes will be based on leaves, with the birds of our land flying around. The pillars of the main nave will be palm trees, the tree of sacrifice, martyrdom and glory. In the lateral naves they will be laurel trees, the tree of wisdom and triumph.

ANTONI GAUDÍ

THE DOME OF THE LATERAL NAVES
A dome with hyperbolic openings to light the inside.

THE GREAT GEOMETRIC FOREST OF THE TEMPLE
The definitive solution to the naves is the epitome of the search for an organic architecture. It comprises twisted forms, helicoids that generate columns and paraboloids and hyperboloids in the walls and domes.

THE FOLIAGE OF A PLANTAIN FOREST
Through the leaves we can see the daylight and, at night, the stars of the firmament.

81

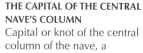

Simple forms are very suitable for decorating; so much so, that it's impossible to create something more harmonious and full of symbolism that the Temple's nave. The central pillars split into five elementary supports that resemble a tree; and these into others, until they reach the highest triforium with the support of the openings emerging from the main pillar. The whole thing composes the last branches of a tree that ascends to the domes: the foliage of that great forest.

ANTONI GAUDÍ

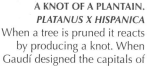

THE CAPITAL OF THE CENTRAL NAVE'S COLUMN

Capital or knot of the central column of the nave, a transition element between the trunk and the branches of that great tree. The geometric solution consists of a main ellipsoid with other smaller ellipsoids intertwined; some of them in reverse that produce intersections decorated with a series of tiny paraboloids.

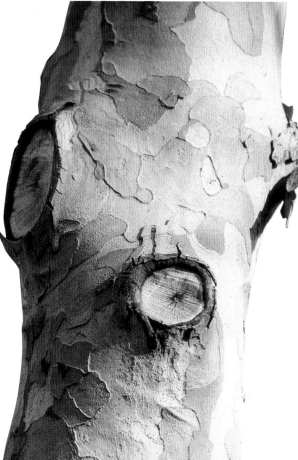

A KNOT OF A PLANTAIN.
PLATANUS X HISPANICA

When a tree is pruned it reacts by producing a knot. When Gaudí designed the capitals of the columns of the main nave of the temple, he added this naturalistic motif.

The pinnacles of the Nativity façade towers

When Gaudí designed the rings or knots in the crowning of the towers of the three temple façades, in the furnishings of the Nativity he opted for polyhedron forms by twinning a cube and an octahedron, as a result of his study of the crystallisation in the polyhedral regular system of some materials, such as the galena, the pyrites, the fluorite and others.

In the knot we find an octahedron with the corners truncated by a cube, resulting in a polyhedron of fourteen sides, six squares, eight irregular hexagons and a sphere with the same centre as the polyhedrons, designing spherical caps that emerge from the sides; everything decorated with Venetian glass tiles enamelled in gold.

THE CRYSTAL TWINNING OF THE PYRITE FE S2
A cubic crystal in the regular system.

THE CRYSTAL TWINNING OF THE PYRITE FE S2
An octahedral crystal in the regular system.

THE PINNACLE OF THE BELL TOWER
The pinnacles of the towers in the Nativity façade, with the knot inspired by the crystallization of minerals. Before he died, Gaudí saw one of them finished.

The tiles that cover the end of the bell tower are made with normal green bottle glass, sturdier than normal glass. Their golden hue is obtained by heating the glass until it starts to melt and once it's extended on the mould, covering it with gold leaf. Since gold melts at a lower temperature than glass, it seeps into it.

These are tiles that could easily be made in Catalonia. This is why I have only ordered the ones I needed for the bell tower; possibly a local glass maker will undertake to make the rest.

If instead of them I had used Manises tiles, this pinnacle would not exhibit the quality it has now; over a clay base the enamel would have melted at a lower temperature. After building the conical crown of the Palacio Güell, I realized that the arrow pinnacles constructed by some architects do not attain the beauty expected of them due to the low quality of the covering and its aspect of terracotta.

ANTONI GAUDÍ

THE CRYSTAL TWINNING OF THE PYRITE FE S2
The crystal twinning of two pyrite cubes.

THE RING OR KNOT OF THE PINNACLE
A polyhedron of fourteen sides, six squares, eight irregular hexagons and spherical caps in relief in the centre of each of the sides.

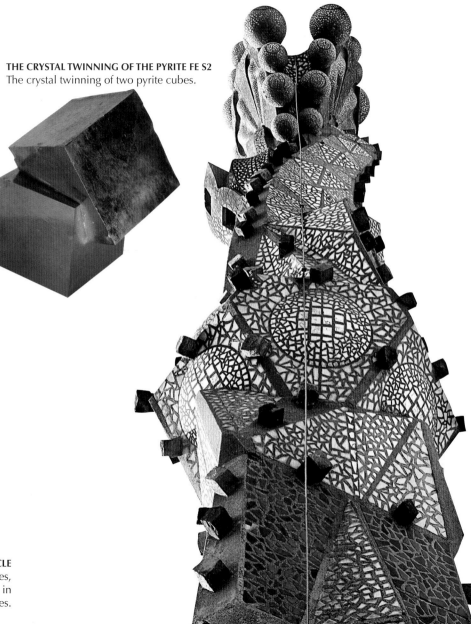

"Look at this ending! Doesn't it seem to unite Heaven and Earth? This outbreak of tiles will be the first thing seen when one approaches Barcelona from the sea, giving one a radiant welcome. I am satisfied with the last models of the Temple naves, but disillusioned at not being able to build a whole stretch of it. I lament the same thing that Da Vinci used to regret: What beautiful things I would make if I had the means to erect them!

ANTONI GAUDÍ

A justified praise. The "bon mot" was pronounced by a simple man: the watchmaker that takes care of rewinding the three clocks of the Sagrada Familia —for an annual salary of 5 duros. He carries out his duty without opening his mouth. But the day he saw the tower freed of its scaffolding he said: "I have seen the finished tower and it's a joy to contemplate". That "it's a joy" sums it all up.

It's the "gaudem magnum" of the Three Wise Men of the Orient, when they saw the star again, which is clarity and, therefore, joy. It's a joy, a pleasure to see. You couldn't say anything better. The man did not resort to trite words; he expressed what he felt. Really, that shining is a joy. And a humble artisan who comes 53 times a year to rewind those three clocks for 25 pesetas has pointed it out.

ANTONI GAUDÍ

THE CRYSTAL TWINNING OF THE PINNACLES
The geometrical figures for the twinning of the pinnacle knot. A cube, an octahedron and a sphere.

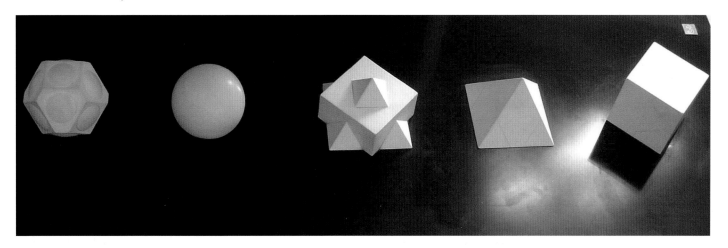

The pinnacle of the clerestory on the lateral Naves facade

In the pinnacle of the clerestory we find the synthesis of the process of analyzing nature, searching for a new organic architecture: the one Gaudí developed and applied in his buildings.

This extraordinary sculpture consists of a geometric basket with eight intertwined paraboloids, filled with fruits rendered in a naturalistic way. In it we have the résumé of Gaudí's architecture and, at the same time, of this book: the naturalistic fruits, the decorative elements of his initial works (Casa Vicens, El Capricho) and the ruled geometry of the ulterior solutions to the naves of the temple.

The decor has been, is, and will be colourful. In nature we never find an object that is monotone and uniform. Everything in vegetation, geology, topography or in the animal kingdom, always maintains a more or less prominent chromatic contrast. For that reason, it's obligatory to colour —totally or in part— any architectural element with iridescences that will perhaps fade, but to which the passage of time will confer a precious patina of its own.

ANTONI GAUDÍ

The Temple is growing slowly, although, as has always been the case with all buildings meant to stand the passage of time, with interruptions. Many years pass before the trunk of a centenary oak attains the width it boasts and, sometimes, a killer frost stops its growth. However, the canes grow quickly but, come autumn, the wind bends them. Sometime ago I read a book about the cathedral of Rheims, the most beautiful of the Gothic temples. I discovered that there was an epoch in which the canons had to travel all over France begging for alms with which to pay for the continuation of the construction works.

ANTONI GAUDÍ

Chronology of Antoni Gaudí: his life and works

Data compiled by the Gaudí Chair, published in the magazine *Temple*

1852, June 25th: At 9:30 am Antoni Gaudí i Cornet was born.

1852, June 26th: He is baptized by *mosén* Josep Casas, vicar of the parish church of Sant Pere de Reus. He receives the names Antón, Plàcid y Guillem, in homage to his father, grandfather and the day's saint.

1860-1862: Attends the elementary school of the teacher Francesc Berenguer, in Reus.

1866: The bishop of Barcelona, Pantaleón Montserrat Navarro, approves the proposal of Josep Maria Bocabella Verdaguer, founding the Asociación de Devotos de San José (Society of Devotes of Saint Joseph).

1863-1867: He starts High School in the Colegio de los Escolapios (Piarists) of Reus, in the old convent of Sant Francesc.

1867, December: The *El Propagador de la Devoción a San José* is published, an official publication of the Asociación de Devotos de San José.

1867: He makes prints using a woodbox plate for the hand-made newspaper *El Arlequín*, with a run of 12 copies. He paints the sets for school representations of the plays *El puñal del godo* y *Don Juan Tenorio* by José Zorrilla.

1868-1869: He studies in the Carmen Street high school of Barcelona.

1870, June: He passes Algebra and Geometry in the Science Department of the University of Barcelona.

1870, July 26th: He illustrates the manuscript of Eduard Toda about Poblet with a drawing of the coat of arms of Abbot Miquel Cuyàs (1752-1764).

1871, June: He passes Calculus and Descriptive Geometry in the Science Department of the University of Barcelona.

1873, May 3rd: Drawing of a leaning solar declining clock. An exercise in the subject of Gnomonics in the Architecture School of Barcelona (Museu Comarcal de Reus).

1873, May: With some other students, he makes a plan of the plot where they want to build the Instituciones Provinciales de Enseñanza en Barcelona (Gaudí Chair).

1873, June 11th: He fails the subject of Drawing in gouache.

1873, November 17th: He fails the subject of Model Making in plaster.

1873: He draws the flag of the Workers Cooperative of Mataró.

1873: Quite probably, he participates in the Project for the Ciudadela Park of Josep Fontserè Mestres.

1874, September 5th: He passes Model Making in plaster.

1874, October 21st: Passes the subjects of Mechanics, Resistance of Materials, Stability, Engines, Water drawing and French.

1874, October 30th: He calculates the materials' resistance for the project of Josep Fontserè for the water tower of the Ciudadela Park, thus passing the subject.

1874, November 17th: He gets into an argument with the Professor August Font and withdraws from the examination of the subject of Projects.

1874: Father Rodríguez describes the temple of Loreto to Gaudí, and suggests that he build a temple in Barcelona, dedicated to the Holy Family.

1875, June 30th: He passes the subject of Projects in the Preparatory Year.

1875, June: He designs the banister of the gazebo for the Municipal Band, now a monument to Bonaventura Carles Aribau.

1875, September: He obtains honours in Projects with the blueprint for "A cemetery door".

1875: He collaborates on the Project for a monumental cascade for the Ciudadela Park, a project of Josep Fontserè Mestres.

1876, March: He makes the plans for a school project in the Spanish Pavilion of the *Centennial Exposition* of Philadelphia (EE.UU.).

1876, March 21st to 30th: (Notes in the diary kept in the Museo Comarcal of Reus.) Gaudí writes that he works as a draughtsman for the Society Padrós & Borràs, in the project for the apse at the Monastery of Montserrat, by order of Francesc de P. Villar i Lozano; in the project for a streetcar for the Villa Arcadia in Montjuïc, for Leandro Serrallach Mas; in the project for a candelabrum for Fontserè and in the cupboard Malera of the Casa Grabulosa and one altar in Masnou.

1876, April 1st to 10th: He works for Fontserè, Villar and Serrallach in the candelabrum, the monastery of Montserrat, the Ateneo Barcelonés, the Vilardell pharmacy and others.

1876, May 30th: He draws the Ciudadela Park's grille for Fontserè, which would be built in the workshop of Nueva Vulcano.

1876, May: He works as a draughtsman in the project for the Natural History Museum of the Ciudadela's Park of Josep Fontserè i Mestres.

1876, June 8th, 13th, 28th and 30th: Gaudí passes Topography, Materials and Art Theory.

1876, July 30th: The engineers Josep Sarramalera and F. de P. Ramis visit Gaudí.

1876, September 8th: Antònia Cornet Bertran, mother of Gaudí, dies.

1876, October 4th: A drawing in the diary of Reus: the problem of homologue polygons.

1876, October 11th: Gaudí obtains honours in Projects with the "Patio for the Excelentísima Diputación" (Gaudí Chair).

1876, November 27th: He misses classes because he's working as draughtsman.

1876, November 28th: The inauguration of the Born Market designed by Josep Maria Fontserè (director of the works), Josep Maria Cornet i Mas (engineer from the Maquinista Terrestre y Marítima) and Antoni Gaudí (apprentice).

1877, January 1st - 6th: Gaudí works with his classmates Ubald Iranzo and Francesc Mariné.

1877, May 28th: Josep M. Bocabella requests from the Town Hall that the Sagrada Familia be declared a public interest construction.

1877, June 14th: Gaudí passes the subjects Urban Hygiene and Policing, Budgeting and Technology.

1877, June 30th: He obtains honours in Projects with "Fountain for the Cataluña Square" (Gaudí Chair).

1878, January 4th: He passes the Validation Exam with the project "Auditorium for the University" (Gaudí Chair).

1878, February 14th: Maria Cornet Bertran, 60 years old and single, Rosa Cornet Bertran, 50 years old (both aunts of Gaudí), Rosa Gaudí Cornet, 40 years old and married (sister of Gaudí) and Antoni Gaudí Cornet, 25 years old and single, all born in Reus and residing in Barcelona, sell the house that used to belong to Anton Cornet Sans and Maria Bertran Buxeda (maternal grandparents of Gaudí), in number 4 of Sant Vicenç Street. J. F. Ràfols in his *Gaudí 1852-1926*, first published in 1929, considers that this was the house where Gaudí was born.

1878, February 15th: Gaudí designs a streetlamp for the Barcelona Town Hall.

1878, March: Pastel drawing of the head of a male goat (Gaudí Chair).

1878, March 15th: Gaudí obtains the title of architect.

1878, March 20th: He requests the return of his school projects from the direction of the Architecture School.

1878, March: He designs homes for the workers of the Mataró Cooperative.

1878, June: Pavilion of the entrance to the Workers Cooperative of Mataró.

1878, August 10th: Text titled "Ornamentation" in the diary of the Reus Museum.

1878, September 22nd: Gaudí designs his work table.

1878: A calling card where he includes his home address, the third floor of the number 11 of Call Street.

1878: A display cabinet for the glove shop of Esteve Comella in the corner of Avinyó and Ferran Streets. It was included in the Universal Exposition of Paris in 1878.

1878: Gaudí designs two stained glass windows for the chapel of a property in Vallgorguina (Vallès Oriental).

1879, April 1st: He designs a grille for the Casa de Pilatos in Sevilla (Nacional Museum of Art of Cataluña).

1879, April 29th: Gaudí is admitted in the Catalan Association of Scientific Excursions, sponsored by Cèsar August Torres Ferreri.

1879, September 24th: The inauguration during the Mercè festivities of the streetlamps of the Plaza Real.

1879, December: Gaudí is named member of the directorate of the Catalan Association of Scientific Excursions. He visits the Round Tower of las Corts de Sarriá.

1880, January 25th: Gaudí visits Santa Maria del Mar. Gaudí is named curator of the Archeology Museum of the Catalan Association of Scientific Excursions.

1880, January 25th: The Association requests that Gaudí dismount the tiles of a house in Bilbao Street and appoints him to a commission for the reform of Barcelona.

1880, October 21st: Decorates the Assembly Hall of the Catalan Association of Scientific Excursions in the third floor of number 10 Paradís Street.

1880, November 20th and 21st: Excursions to Vilafranca del Penedès and Olesa de Bonesvalls.

1881, January 2nd and February 4th: He published an article in the newspaper *La Renaixença*, about the Decorative Arts Exposition.

1881, January 19th: With Torrents and Rossinyol, he designs the coat of arms of the Catalan Association of Scientific Excursions.

1881, June: He presents the project 'a pavilion-dining room for the visit of King Alfonso XII to Comillas', constructed in the workshop of Eudald Puntí, to be installed in the garden of the Finca Güell.

1881, August: General plans of the Workers Cooperative of Mataró.

1881, December 31th: Josep M. Bocabella buys the plot between Provença, Marina, Mallorca and Sardenya Streets, in Sant Martí de Provençals, where the Sagrada Familia temple will be built.

1882, March 19th: The bishop of Barcelona Josep Urquinaona Bidot sets the first stone of the Sagrada Familia. The original project was made by the architect of the diocese Francesc de P. Villar i Lozano.

1882, May 18th: An excursion to the Monastery of Poblet. Nocturnal lighting of the ruins.

1882: Gaudí participates in the project for the Salesas Church (of Joan MartorellI, in Paseo de San Juan Street.

1882: He designs the hunting pavilion in Garraf for Eusebi Güell.

1883, February 26th: Gaudí designs a house for Manuel Vicens Montaner in Sant Gervasi Street (now, Carolines Street), in the Gracia neighbourhood.

1883: Máximo Díaz de Quijano entrusts Gaudí with the design of El Capricho, in Comillas.

1883, July: Bleaching room for the Workers Cooperative of Mataró.

1883, July: Blueprint for the chapel of the Holy Sacrament for the parish church of Sant Fèlix d'Alella (Maresme). Short stays during the summer in the house of the Vicens family in Dalt Street (today, Anselm Clavé Street). Drawing of a fireplace (Casa-Museo Gaudí) and of a corner cupboard (descendents of Manuel Vicens).

1883, October 20th: The Gracia Town Hall allows Manuel Vicens Montaner to build a cascade in the garden of his house in Sant Gervasi Street.

1883, November 3rd: He intervenes in the Expiatory Temple of the Sagrada Familia for the first time.

1884, March 18th: Gaudí fires the contractor of the Sagrada Familia, Macario Planella Roura.

1884, June: Flag for the Workers Cooperative of Mataró.

1884, November 22nd: *Mossèn* Cinto Verdaguer commissions the canon Jaume Colell Vancells to write a Latin motto for the Fountain of Hercules and the dragon that Gaudí is building for the garden of the Finca Güell.

1884, December: Project of the altar of Saint Joseph for the crypt of the Sagrada Familia.

1884-1887: Gaudí reforms Casa Güell in las Corts de Sarriá: door of the Dragon, porter's lodge, stables, belvedere, porch, Hercules fountain, door knocker and side doors.

1885, March: He presents the blueprints for the ground floor of the Sagrada Familia in the Town Hall of Sant Martí de Provençals.

1885, July: Décor of the bleaching room of the Workers Cooperative of Mataró for a party.

1886, June 30th: Project of the Palacio Güell in number 3 of the Conde del Asalto Street (now Nou de la Rambla) (1886-1888).

1887, June: Project of the Episcopal Palace of Astorga, entrusted to Gaudí by the bishop Joan Grau Vallespinós.

1887: Offices of the Sagrada Familia.

1888, April: Gaudí presents a project for the Universal Exposition of Barcelona and reforms the Pavilion of the Compañía Trasatlántica, in the Maritime section.

1888, June: Pushed by Father Enric d'Ossó Cervelló, now Saint Enric d'Ossó, Gaudí assumes the direction of the Works in the Teresianas School of Ganduxer Street.

1888, October 19th: Setting of the First Stone of the above project, designed by J. B. Pons Trabal.

1889, June 24th: Setting of the First Stone of the Episcopal Palace of Astorga.

1889: Closing of the vault of the crypt in the Sagrada Familia.

1891: Second project for the Sagrada Familia.

1892, April 22th: Josep M. Bocabella i Verdaguer dies.

1892: Studies of the Nativity's façade for the Sagrada Familia.

1892-1893: Project of the Franciscan Catholic Missions in Tangiers.

1892-1894: House of the Botines and square of San Marcelo, in León.

1894: Gaudí finishes the work on the apse of the Sagrada Familia and the foundations of the Nativity façade.

1895, January 14th: Project of the Cellar Güell in Garraf (Sitges).

1896: Construction of the middle column in the Nativity Portico, with Christ's genealogy sculpted in it. He begins the cloister of the Sagrada Familia.

1897: He finishes the construction of the Cellar Güell in Garraf (Sitges) and inaugurates the Isabel bell of the chapel.

1898-1899: Casa Calvet in the number 48 of Casp Street.

1898: Cast iron lectern and cupboard for the sacristy of the Sagrada Familia.

1898: Preliminary studies for the church of the Colonia Güell in Santa Coloma de Cervelló.

1899: Installation of the seraphim with trumpets in the façade of the Sagrada Familia.

1900, June 11th: The Town Hall awards the prize Best Building of the Year to Casa Calvet.

1900, October: Levelling of the trails in Parque Güell. That December they found the cave of fossils.

1900-1909: Casa Bellesguard in Sant Gervasi de Cassoles.

1900-1902: Door and fence of the house of Hermenegild Miralles. Private road Güell, now Manuel Girona Street.

1900-1914: Parque Güell. Urbanization of Mount Pelada in the Salut neighbourhood of Gràcia. Imperial staircase, column hall, Greek theatre, and viaducts. Way of the Cross, house where Gaudí lived from 1906 to 1925.

1901: Project for a monumental cross with the symbols of the Passion for the Parque Güell.

1902: Model of the Flight to Egypt for the Nativity Portico of the Sagrada Familia.

1902-1904: Sample house for the Parque Güell, following the project of Francesc Berenguer Mestres.

1902: Gaudí decorates the saloon Torino, a bar in Passeig de Gràcia Street.

1903-1914: Restoration of Mallorca's cathedral. They move the choirs, the canopy, the bay windows, the main altar, the pulpits and the sepulchres of the Kings of Mallorca.

1903: Model for the group *The Killing of the Innocents* for the Nativity façade of the Sagrada Familia.

1904-1906: He reforms Casa Batlló in number 43 of Passeig de Gràcia Street.

1904: Alfonso XIII visits the Sagrada Familia, where Gaudí explains his Project to him.

1905: Gaudí buys the model house of Parque Güell, as a home for his father, his niece Rosa and himself.

1905-1907: Artigas Gardens in Pobla de Lillet.

1906, January 20th: For the first time, the newspaper *La Veu de Catalunya* published a sketch of the Sagrada Familia complex drawn by "one of his admirers" and approved by Gaudí.

1906, February 2nd: Project for Casa Milà.

1906, March 18th: In *La Ilustració Catalana*, the architect Joan Rubió Bellver published another sketch of the Sagrada Familia.

1906, October 13th: Casa Batlló is finished.

1906, October 29th: Francesc Gaudí i Serra, Gaudí's father, dies.

1906-1911: Casa de Rosario Segimon Artells y Pere Milà i Camps, called La Pedrera, in number 92 of the Passeig de Gràcia Street.

1907: The Sagrada Familia becomes a parish.

1908, May 18th: He begins the detour of the Bellesguard trail. The work is completed by August 14th.

1908, May 20th: Gaudí extends a certificate of professional competence to Domènec Sugrañes.

1908: Project of the chapel of the Teresianas School.

1908, May: Draft of the Hotel Atracción in New York.

1908, October 4th: Setting of the First Stone for the church of the Colonia Güell in Santa Coloma de Cervelló. Gaudí calculates the structures with a stereoscopic model and little bags of pellets. Only the crypt was built.

1909, March: He finishes the plaster model of *The Virgen and the Archangels*, of Carles Mani Roig, which will be cast in bronze for the Pedrera's façade.

1909: The Sagrada Familia schools.

1909: A plaster model (painted over by J. M. Jujol Gibert) of the Nativity façade of the Sagrada Familia, for a Gaudí show in Paris.

1910, March-April: Gaudí Exposition in the Grand Palais of Paris, organized by Eusebi Güell.

1910, December 22nd: Gaudí signs the certificate of fitness for the main floor of Casa Milà.

1910: A streetlight in homage to Jaume Balmes in Vic, with the collaboration of Pericas and Jujol.

1911, June 9th: Gaudí catches the Maltese fevers and moves to the Hotel Europa of Puigcerdà, accompanied by Doctor Pere Santaló. He draws his first will, signed in front of Ramon Cantó, notary of Puigcerdà.

1911, October: Project of the Passion's façade for the Sagrada Familia.

1912, October 31st: Gaudí certifies the ending of the construction of La Pedrera.

1912: Pulpits for the parish church of Blanes.

1913, April: Professor Fèlix Cardellach and his students of the Engineering School visit the Works of the crypt of the Colonia Güell.

1914, February 10th: Francesc Berenguer Mestres (Reus, 21/7/1866), his assistant, dies.

1914, April 14th: Gaudí approves the bill of the carpenter Tomàs Bernat for making 20 benches for the church of the Colonia Güell.

1915: The bishop of Barcelona Enric Reig Casanova and the president of the Catalonia Mancomunitat Enric Prat de la Riba visit the works of the Sagrada Familia.

1915, February 16th: Professor Fèlix Cardellach and his students of the Engineering School visit the Sagrada Familia again. On February 25th, Cardellach publishes an interesting article about the temple in *La Vanguardia*.

1915, March 21th: The president of the Architects' Association of Catalonia, Bonaventura Bassegoda Amigó, and a group of its members visit the Sagrada Familia invited by Gaudí, who wants to thank them for the 1.212 pesetas they have collected to continue the works.

1915: The *Album of the Sagrada Familia* is published in five languages.

1915: Trial test with tubular bells in the Sagrada Familia.

1915: Gaudí visits the offices of the Architects' Association of Catalonia to show his gratitude for their donations.

1916, June: The architect Guillem Reynés Font makes a drawing of the models for the tombs of kings Jaume II y III made by Gaudí, to be sent to Alfonso XIII.

1916: Project for a monument for the recently deceased bishop of Vic, Josep Torras i Bages, to be erected in front of the Passion façade.

1916: Princess Isabel visits the Sagrada Familia.

1916: Gaudí takes a course in Gregorian chanting in the Orfeó Català, directed by the Benedictine monk Father Sunyol.

1917: Topographic plan and views of the Sagrada Familia. Gaudí objects to the Accesses Plan of Léon Jaussely formulated by the Town Hall.

1917: Outline of a monument dedicated to Enric Prat de la Riba in Castelltterçol. Lluís Bonet i Garí designs the project.

1919: Model of the sacristy of the Sagrada Familia.

1922, July 21th: The Holy See's nuncio to Spain, Monsignor Federico Tedeschini, visits the Sagrada Familia. Gaudí explains the meaning of the seven doors in the Glory façade to him.

1922: He offers Father Aranda the possibility of using the chapel of the Virgin of the Angels (behind the apse of the Sagrada Familia) as a model for the construction of a chapel in Rancagua (Chile).

1922: The National Congress of Spanish Architects approves a motion of commendation of Gaudí.

1923: He finishes the model for the sacristy of the Sagrada Familia.

1924, June 16th: He takes part in the procession of Corpus with the Círculo Artístico de Sant Lluch. Branguli takes a picture of him as he's leaving the cathedral.

1924: Installation of the group of sculptures *The killing of the Innocents* in the Sagrada Familia.

1925, January: Gaudí leaves the house in Parque Güell and goes to live in the Sagrada Familia.

1925, January: Gaudí cedes his land in Riudoms to the Archbishop of Tarragona and the shares in the dam of Riudecanyes, to fund a Benedit in memory of his father and his niece in Sant Jaume or in the chapel of Sant Antoni of Riudoms, for the prayer of the Spiritual Visit to the Virgin of Montserrat, written by the bishop Josep Torras i Bages.

1925, January: Gaudí donates his bonds in the railway from Almansa to Tarragona to the Archbishop of Tarragona, to fund a similar benefit in memory of his mother, in Sant Pere of Reus.

1925, November 30th: End of the works of the bell tower of Saint Bernabé in the Sagrada Familia.

1926, June 7th: At the intersection of Gran Vía and Bailén Streets, Gaudí gets run over by a streetcar.

1926, June 10th: Gaudí dies.

1926, June 12th: Gaudí is buried in the Carmen chapel in the crypt of the Sagrada Familia.

1926, November 16th: His executors carry out his last will; giving the house in Parque Güell and 3.000 pesetas he had in the Caixa de Pensions and the Banco de España to the Sagrada Familia.

1927, July 29th: Llorenç Matamala i Piñol, head of the model workshop of the Sagrada Familia, dies.

1936, July 20th: The revolutionary hordes burn the crypt and destroy the archives.

1939, January 26th: When Franco's troops enter Barcelona, the work of recuperating the Sagrada Familia begins.

1939, December: Gaudí's assistants identify his body which had been thrown out of the tomb in 1938.

Biographical data of the author

Jordi Cussó i Anglès was born in Barcelona on May 11th of 1942 and was baptized in the Rosary chapel, in the first northern stretch of the cloister of the Sagrada Familia, where, after the burning of the crypt in July of 1936, they rehabilitated a space for the celebration of weddings and baptisms.

The fact that he lived no further than a stone's throw from the Sagrada Familia, meant that as a child he played in the fields in front of the Nativity façade, between stones and sculptures that would not be incorporated into the temple until years later.

In 1951 he received his First Communion in the already restored crypt. He took part in the parish's activities, as carrier of the image of Christ, stagehand for the Theatre's group and even as an actor. With his parents, he collaborated year after year in the solicitation of funds for the temple's construction, in several ways: by dancing with a group in front of the petition tables to attract the public and, later on, presiding over one of them.

In November of 1957, he entered the model workshop as an apprentice. Ten years later he was made the director of it. He intervened in the gathering, study and restoration of the original Gaudí's models destroyed during the Spanish Civil War.

Searching for his family's roots, in 1988 he moved to the Maresme: Cabrera de Mar first and Sant Iscle de Vallalta, later. There he lived surrounded by hills, taking care of a small garden. This led to his first experiences as an amateur naturalist, searching for the organic forms so masterly reproduced by Gaudí.

On February 19th of 1991, the Honourable Jordi Pujol i Soley, President of the Generalitat of Catalonia gave him the title of Master Artisan.

In 2002, the Mayor of Sant Iscle de Vallalta, Eduard Tron i Mainat, convoked a meeting to promote the cultural activities of the town, in which it was suggested that an exposition about Gaudí be made, directed by Jordi Cussó, an enthusiast of the project. After some time, he presented a series of pictures about Gaudí's work, ordered chronologically, on which he intercalated comparative images of the vegetal and animal realms, models, objects and live plants.

Antoní Gaudí studied and incorporated his intense observation of nature. His objective was to urge the viewers to look at nature through Gaudí's eyes. The Town Hall approved his proposal on August 2nd of that year, the International Year of Gaudí. The exposition *Gaudir de la natura* ("The Joy of nature") was staged in the cultural centre of the town, during its annual feast. The show travelled to Arenys de Mar, Mataró and Cabrera de Mar, and from June of 2003 stayed for five years in the Museum of the Temple of the Sagrada Familia. It was one of the expositions that drew the most visitors in the whole country.

On May 11th of 2006, alter working for nearly fifty years in the Sagrada Familia, he retired. It's not likely that this will mean the end of his investigations; most probably he will keep on collaborating with the temple, preparing the materials to divulge what he has learned.

As a result of this collaboration, on June 17th of 2008 the permanent exposition *GAUDÍ & NATURA* was inaugurated in the cloister of Montserrat, next to the Nativity façade; an exhibition that takes into consideration the access of blind and disabled persons.

Bibliography

Bassegoda, J., *El Gran Gaudí*, Ausa Ed., Sabadell, 1989.

Bonet, J., *El último Gaudí*, Pòrtic, Barcelona, 2001.

Gómez, J.; Coll, J.; Melero, J. i Burry, M., *La Sagrada Família. De Gaudí al CAD*, UPC, 1996.

Puig Boada, I., *El Templo de la Sagrada Familia*, editorial Omega, Barcelona, 1952.

Giralt-Miracle, D. (dir.), *Gaudí, 2002. Miscelánea*, Planeta, Barcelona, 2002.

Giralt-Miracle, D. (dir.), *Gaudí. La búsqueda de la forma*, Lunwerg Editores, Barcelona, 2002.